Security and Vulnerability Assessment

EC-Council | Press

Volume 5 of 5 mapping to

E|NSA™

EC-Council | **Network Security
Administrator**

Certification

COURSE TECHNOLOGY
CENGAGE Learning™

Australia • Brazil • Japan • Korea • Mexico • Singapore • Spain • United Kingdom • United States

COURSE TECHNOLOGY
CENGAGE Learning™

Security and Vulnerability Assessment:
EC-Council | Press

Course Technology/Cengage Learning
  Staff:

Vice President, Career and Professional
  Editorial: Dave Garza

Director of Learning Solutions:
  Matthew Kane

Executive Editor: Stephen Helba

Managing Editor: Marah Bellegarde

Editorial Assistant: Meghan Orvis

Vice President, Career and Professional
  Marketing: Jennifer Ann Baker

Marketing Director: Deborah Yarnell

Marketing Manager: Erin Coffin

Marketing Coordinator: Shanna Gibbs

Production Director: Carolyn Miller

Production Manager: Andrew Crouth

Content Project Manager:
  Brooke Greenhouse

Senior Art Director: Jack Pendleton

EC-Council:

President | EC-Council: Sanjay Bavisi

Sr. Director US | EC-Council:
  Steven Graham

For product information and technology assistance, contact us at
Cengage Learning Customer & Sales Support, 1-800-354-9706

For permission to use material from this text or product,
submit all requests online at **www.cengage.com/permissions**.
Further permissions questions can be e-mailed to
permissionrequest@cengage.com

Library of Congress Control Number: 2010924897

ISBN-13: 978-1-4354-8359-0

ISBN-10: 1-4354-8359-6

Cengage Learning
5 Maxwell Drive
Clifton Park, NY 12065-2919
USA

Cengage Learning is a leading provider of customized learning solutions with office locations around the globe, including Singapore, the United Kingdom, Australia, Mexico, Brazil, and Japan. Locate your local office at: **international.cengage.com/region**

Cengage Learning products are represented in Canada by
Nelson Education, Ltd.

For more learning solutions, please visit our corporate website at **www.cengage.com**

NOTICE TO THE READER

Printed in the United States of America
2 3 4 5 6 7   15 14 13

TABLE OF CONTENTS v

PREFACE xiii

CHAPTER 1
Web Security 1-1

CHAPTER 2
E-Mail Security 2-1

CHAPTER 3
Authentication, Encryption, and Digital Signatures 3-1

CHAPTER 4
Virtual Private Networks 4-1

CHAPTER 5
Creating Fault Tolerance 5-1

CHAPTER 6
Incident Response 6-1

CHAPTER 7
Disaster Recovery Planning and Risk Analysis 7-1

CHAPTER 8
Network Vulnerability Assessment 8-1

INDEX I-1

Table of Contents

PREFACE xi

CHAPTER 1

Web Security 1-1

  Objectives 1-1

  Key Terms 1-1

  Introduction to Web Security 1-1

  Web Architecture 1-1

  Common Threats on the Web 1-2

    Identity Theft 1-2

    Spam 1-2

    Distributed Denial-Of-Service Attack 1-3

    Parasitic Malware 1-4

    Bots 1-4

    Cross-Site Request Forgery 1-4

    Session Hijacking 1-4

    Smurf Attack 1-4

    FTP Bounce 1-4

    RSS/Atomic Injection 1-5

    DNS Attack 1-5

    Content Spoofing 1-5

    Logical Attacks 1-5

    Buffer Overflow 1-5

    IP and Routing Protocol Spoofing 1-6

  Identifying Unauthorized Network Devices 1-6

    Restrictive Access 1-6

    Network Addresses 1-7

    Installing and Protecting IIS 1-8

  Client Authorization 1-8

    Certificate Authorities 1-8

    Client-Side Data 1-8

    Server-Side Data 1-9

    User Approaches 1-10

    Authentication Techniques 1-10

    Input Data Validation 1-11

  Deploying and Managing Web-Based Solutions 1-11

    Browsing Analysis 1-11

    Browser Security 1-12

    Browser Hijacking 1-12

    Browser Behavior Analysis 1-14

    Dynamic Code 1-14

  Plug-Ins 1-14

    Adobe Shockwave and Flash 1-15

    Apple QuickTime 1-15

    Java 1-15

    Mozilla Firefox Extensions 1-15

    Adobe Reader 1-15

    Windows Media Player 1-15

    Validate Sites HTML 1-15

    Validate P3P 1-15

    View-In 1-16

    BugMeNot 1-16

    Webpage Speed Report 1-16

    Validate Links (W3C) 1-16

    Open Text 1-16

    Validate RSS 1-16

    Validate CSS 1-16

  Common Gateway Interface (CGI) 1-16

    CGI Script 1-17

    Mechanisms and Variables 1-17

    Third-Party CGI Scripts 1-17

    Server Side Includes (SSIs) 1-18

CGI Operation 1-18

Responding to the Client 1-18

Using the Client to Call a CGI Application 1-19

Chapter Summary 1-19

Review Questions 1-20

Hands-On Projects 1-22

CHAPTER 2
E-Mail Security **2-1**

Objectives 2-1

Key Terms 2-1

Introduction to E-Mail Security 2-1

Elements of E-Mail 2-2

POP3 Versus Web-Based E-Mail. 2-2

POP3 E-Mail 2-2

Web-Based E-Mail. 2-2

E-Mail Components 2-3

Header 2-3

Attachments. 2-6

Signatures 2-6

Configuring and Testing an E-Mail Server. 2-7

UNIX E-Mail Server 2-7

Microsoft Exchange 2000 E-Mail Server 2-7

Novell GroupWise E-Mail Server 2-7

E-Mail Encryption and Authentication 2-7

CenturionMail. 2-7

Kerberos. 2-8

Hushmail 2-8

Pretty Good Privacy (PGP) 2-8

Secure Hive 2-8

Softalk WorkgroupMail 2-9

Configuring Outlook Express. 2-13

E-Mail Protocols. 2-13

Multipurpose Internet Mail Extensions (MIME)/Secure MIME 2-14

Pretty Good Privacy (PGP) 2-14

Simple Mail Transfer Protocol (SMTP) 2-14

Internet Message Access Protocol (IMAP) 2-14

Post Office Protocol Version 3 (POP3) 2-14

Client-Server Architecture 2-15

Client-Server Architecture in a LAN. 2-15

Client-Server Architecture in the Internet 2-15

E-Mail Security Risks 2-15

Spam 2-15

Hoaxes. 2-16

Phishing 2-16

Snarfing 2-17

Malware. 2-17

E-Mail Spoofing 2-18

Attachment Security 2-18

E-Mail Bombing 2-20

Increasing E-Mail Security 2-20

Quarantining Suspicious E-Mail 2-20

Vulnerability Checks 2-20

Tools for E-Mail Security 2-21

Tracking an E-Mail. 2-24

ReadNotify 2-24

Chapter Summary 2-25

Review Questions 2-25

Hands-On Projects 2-27

CHAPTER 3
Authentication, Encryption, and Digital Signatures **3-1**

Objectives 3-1

Key Terms 3-1

Introduction to Authentication, Encryption, and Digital Signatures 3-2

Authentication 3-2
    RSA SecurID 3-2
    Smart Cards. 3-2
    VeriSign Authentication. 3-2
    Authenticating Network Clients 3-2

Encryption 3-3
    Implementing Encryption in Firewalls. 3-3
    Cost of Firewall Encryption 3-4
    Preserving Data Integrity. 3-4
    Maintaining Confidentiality 3-4
    Message Authentication. 3-4
    Strength 3-5
    Hashing Algorithms. 3-5
    Encryption Algorithms 3-5
    Analyzing Popular Encryption Schemes 3-6

IPSec 3-10
    IPSec Protocols 3-10
    IPSec Implementation 3-11
    IPSec Components 3-12
    IPSec Modes 3-13
    IPSec Configuration. 3-13
    Internet Key Exchange (IKE) Security Associations 3-14
    IPSec Processing Steps 3-14
    IPSec Algorithms 3-14
    IPSec Policies 3-14
    IPSec Limitations. 3-15

Digital Certificates 3-15
    Standards for Digital Certificates 3-15
    X.509 as Authentication Standard 3-16
    Public-Key Certificate 3-16
    Viewing Digital Certificates 3-16

Digital Signatures 3-16
    Private-Key Infrastructure (PKI) 3-17

Chapter Summary. 3-18

Review Questions 3-18

Hands-On Projects 3-20

CHAPTER 4
Virtual Private Networks **4-1**

Objectives 4-1

Key Terms 4-1

Introduction to Virtual Private Networks 4-2

VPN Classification 4-2
    Internal LAN VPNs. 4-2
    Remote Access VPNs. 4-2
    Extranet VPNs. 4-2

Tunneling 4-2
    Types of Tunneling. 4-3
    VPN Tunneling Protocols 4-4

VPN Security. 4-6
    Client Privacy. 4-6
    Data Reliability 4-6
    Information Authenticity. 4-6

VPN Connection. 4-7
    SSH and PPP 4-7
    Concentrator 4-7

Setting Up a VPN 4-7

Implementing VPN Servers 4-9
    Implementing DHCP Service 4-9
    Creating an Enterprise Certificate Authority 4-11
    Installing IAS 4-11
    Configuring IAS 4-11
    Creating a Remote Access Policy 4-12
    Configuring the Remote Access Server as a Router 4-12
    Associating the VPN Server with the DHCP Server 4-12
    Configuring Remote Clients 4-13
    Testing the Client Connection 4-13

VPN Policies 4-13
    VPN Registration and Passwords 4-13

VPN Troubleshooting 4-13
    VPN Risks 4-13
    Implementation Review 4-14

VPN Product Testing 4-16
    Common VPN Flaws 4-17
    Insecure Storage of Authentication Credentials by VPN Clients 4-17
    Username Enumeration Vulnerabilities 4-18
    Man-In-The-Middle Attacks 4-20
    Lack of Account Lockout 4-20
    Poor Default Configurations 4-20
    Poor Guidance and Documentation 4-20

Chapter Summary 4-21

Review Questions 4-21

Hands-On Projects 4-23

CHAPTER 5
Creating Fault Tolerance **5-1**

Objectives 5-1

Key Terms 5-1

Introduction to Creating Fault Tolerance 5-2

Planning for Fault Tolerance 5-2
    Aspects of Fault Tolerance 5-2

Reasons for System Failure 5-2
    Crime 5-2
    User Error 5-3
    Environment 5-3
    Routine Events 5-4

Preventive Measures 5-4
    Backup 5-5
    UPSs and Power Generators 5-6
    Perimeter Security 5-6
    Physical Security 5-7
    Offsite Storage 5-7
    Redundant Array of Independent Disks (RAID) 5-7
    Clustered Servers 5-10
    Simple Server Redundancy 5-11
    Archiving 5-12
    Circuit Redundancy 5-12

Deployment Testing 5-12

Chapter Summary 5-13

Review Questions 5-13

Hands-On Projects 5-15

CHAPTER 6
Incident Response **6-1**

Objectives 6-1

Key Terms 6-1

Introduction to Incident Response 6-1

Classification of Incidents. 6-1
    Categories 6-2
    Types of Incidents 6-2

Reporting Incidents. 6-3
    Contact Personnel 6-3
    What to Report 6-3
    Step-By-Step Procedure 6-3
    Incident Reporting Forms 6-5

Incident Management 6-6
    Surviving Large Incidents 6-6
    Assigning Ownership. 6-6
    Preparing Tracking Charts 6-6
    Assigning Priorities to Incidents 6-6

Incident Response Architecture 6-6

Six-Step Approach to Incident Handling 6-7
    Preparation 6-8
    Detection 6-8
    Containment 6-9
    Eradication 6-10
    Recovery 6-10
    Follow-Up 6-10

Computer Security Incident Response Team (CSIRT) 6-11
    Functional Requirements. 6-11
    Methods of Communication 6-12
    Staffing Issues 6-12
    Incident Response Team Life Cycle 6-12
    Obstacles in Building a Successful Response Team 6-12
    Services Provided 6-13

Chapter Summary. 6-14

Review Questions 6-14

Hands-On Projects 6-16

CHAPTER 7
Disaster Recovery Planning and Risk Analysis. **7-1**

Objectives 7-1

Key Terms 7-1

Introduction to Disaster Recovery Planning and Risk Analysis 7-1

Disaster Recovery Overview 7-2
    Principles of Disaster Recovery 7-2
    Business Process Inventory 7-2
    Backups 7-2

Disaster Recovery Planning 7-4
    Security Planning. 7-4
    Budget Planning. 7-5
    Disaster Recovery Planning Process 7-5

Risk Analysis. 7-8
    Potential Threats 7-8
    Methods of Risk Analysis 7-8
    Risk Management 7-9
    Roles and Responsibilities in Risk Analysis. 7-10
    Risk Analysis Results Evaluation. 7-11

Myths About Disaster Recovery 7-11
    One Recovery Plan Can Meet All Requirements. 7-11
    The More Distance Between the Primary Site and Backup Site, the Better the Protection 7-11
    A Combined Approach Must Be Followed to Allow for Business Continuity Planning and Testing. . . . 7-11
    Data Recovery Restricts Data Losses to a Minimum 7-11
    Maintaining a Copy of Mirrored Data Is Sufficient at Recovery Site 7-11
    A Large Amount of Bandwidth Is Required for Remote Backups 7-12

Chapter Summary. 7-12

Review Questions 7-12

Hands-On Projects 7-13

CHAPTER 8
Network Vulnerability Assessment **8-1**

　Objectives 8-1

　Key Terms 8-1

　Introduction to Network Vulnerability Assessment 8-1

　Vulnerability Assessment Services 8-2
　　Network Vulnerability Assessment Timeline 8-2
　　Network Vulnerability Assessment Team 8-2
　　Vulnerability Types 8-3
　　Goals of Vulnerability Assessment 8-3

　Network Vulnerability Assessment Methodology 8-3
　　Phase I: Data Collection 8-3
　　Phase II: Identification 8-4
　　Phase III: Analysis 8-5
　　Phase IV: Evaluation 8-5
　　Phase V: Generation 8-5

　Vulnerability Assessment Tools 8-5
　　SAINT 8-6
　　Nessus 8-6
　　BindView 8-7
　　Nmap 8-7
　　Ethereal 8-7
　　Retina Network Security Scanner 8-8
　　Sandcat 8-8
　　VForce 8-8
　　ScanIT Online 8-8

　Chapter Summary 8-9

　Review Questions 8-9

　Hands-On Projects 8-10

INDEX **I-1**

Hacking and electronic crimes sophistication has grown at an exponential rate in recent years. In fact, recent reports have indicated that cyber crime already surpasses the illegal drug trade! Unethical hackers better known as *black hats* are preying on information systems of government, corporate, public, and private networks and are constantly testing the security mechanisms of these organizations to the limit with the sole aim of exploiting it and profiting from the exercise. High profile crimes have proven that the traditional approach to computer security is simply not sufficient, even with the strongest perimeter, properly configured defense mechanisms like firewalls, intrusion detection, and prevention systems, strong end-to-end encryption standards, and anti-virus software. Hackers have proven their dedication and ability to systematically penetrate networks all over the world. In some cases *black hats* may be able to execute attacks so flawlessly that they can compromise a system, steal everything of value, and completely erase their tracks in less than 20 minutes!

The EC-Council Press is dedicated to stopping hackers in their tracks.

About EC-Council

The International Council of Electronic Commerce Consultants, better known as EC-Council was founded in late 2001 to address the need for well-educated and certified information security and e-business practitioners. EC-Council is a global, member-based organization comprised of industry and subject matter experts all working together to set the standards and raise the bar in information security certification and education.

EC-Council first developed the *Certified Ethical Hacker,* C|EH program. The goal of this program is to teach the methodologies, tools, and techniques used by hackers. Leveraging the collective knowledge from hundreds of subject matter experts, the C|EH program has rapidly gained popularity around the globe and is now delivered in over 70 countries by over 450 authorized training centers. Over 80,000 information security practitioners have been trained.

C|EH is the benchmark for many government entities and major corporations around the world. Shortly after C|EH was launched, EC-Council developed the *Certified Security Analyst,* E|CSA. The goal of the E|CSA program is to teach groundbreaking analysis methods that must be applied while conducting advanced penetration testing. E|CSA leads to the *Licensed Penetration Tester,* L|PT status. The *Computer Hacking Forensic Investigator,* C|HFI was formed with the same design methodologies above and has become a global standard in certification for computer forensics. EC-Council through its impervious network of professionals, and huge industry following has developed various other programs in information security and e-business. EC-Council Certifications are viewed as the essential certifications needed where standard configuration and security policy courses fall short. Providing a true, hands-on, tactical approach to security, individuals armed with the knowledge disseminated by EC-Council programs are securing networks around the world and beating the hackers at their own game.

About the EC-Council | Press

The EC-Council | Press was formed in late 2008 as a result of a cutting edge partnership between global information security certification leader, EC-Council and leading global academic publisher, Cengage Learning. This partnership marks a revolution in academic textbooks and courses of study in Information Security, Computer Forensics, Disaster Recovery, and End-User Security. By identifying the essential topics and content of EC-Council professional certification programs, and repurposing this world class content to fit academic programs, the EC-Council | Press was formed. The academic community is now able to incorporate this powerful cutting edge content into new and existing Information Security programs. By closing the gap between academic study and professional certification, students and instructors are able to leverage the power of rigorous academic focus and high demand industry certification. The EC-Council | Press is set to revolutionize global information security programs and ultimately create a new breed of practitioners capable of combating the growing epidemic of cybercrime and the rising threat of cyber-war.

Network Defense Series

The EC-Council | Press *Network Defense* series, preparing learners for E|NSA certification, is intended for those studying to become secure system administrators, network security administrators and anyone who is interested in network security technologies. This series is designed to educate learners, from a vendor neutral standpoint, how to defend the networks they manage. This series covers the fundamental skills in evaluating internal and external threats to network security, design, and how to enforce network level security policies, and ultimately protect an organization's information. Covering a broad range of topics from secure network fundamentals, protocols & analysis, standards and policy, hardening infrastructure, to configuring IPS, IDS and firewalls, bastion host and honeypots, among many other topics, learners completing this series will have a full understanding of defensive measures taken to secure their organizations information. The series when used in its entirety helps prepare readers to take and succeed on the E|NSA, Network Security Administrator certification exam from EC-Council.

Books in Series
- *Network Defense: Fundamentals and Protocols*/1435483553
- *Network Defense: Security Policy and Threats*/1435483561
- *Network Defense: Perimeter Defense Mechanisms*/143548357X
- *Network Defense: Securing and Troubleshooting Network Operating Systems*/1435483588
- *Network Defense: Security and Vulnerability Assessment*/1435483596

Security and Vulnerability Assessment

Security and Vulnerability Assessment includes coverage of web and e-mail security; the use of authentication, encryption and digital signatures; fundamentals of virtual private networks, how to create fault tolerance, how to execute an incident response, disaster recover plan and how to implement a risk analysis; and how to perform a vulnerability assessment of a network.

Chapter Contents:

Chapter 1, *Web Security*, discusses the great concern surrounding web security and how to secure Web Servers, clients, and networks. Chapter 2, *E-Mail Security*, familiarizes the reader with the important elements of e-mail and how to send and receive e-mails safely and securely. Chapter 3, *Authentication, Encryption and Digital Signatures*, explains several techniques being used to authenticate users and encrypt data and introduces the concept of digital signatures. Chapter 4, *Virtual Private Networks*, discusses the basics of Virtual Private Networks, including how they work and how to implement them. Chapter 5, *Creating Fault Tolerance*, explains to ensure that systems are capable of recovering from any unpredicted hardware, software or power failures. Chapter 6, *Incident Response*, explains how to recognize, report, and respond to incidents in order to minimize damage and resume normal operations, Chapter 7, *Disaster Recovery Planning and Risk Analysis*, discusses how to plan and execute effective disaster recovery methodologies and how to analyze risk before a disaster occurs. Chapter 8, *Network Vulnerability Assessment*, explains how to conduct assessment of a network.

Chapter Features

Many features are included in each chapter and all are designed to enhance the learner's learning experience. Features include:

- *Objectives* begin each chapter and focus the learner on the most important concepts in the chapter.
- *Key Terms* are designed to familiarize the learner with terms that will be used within the chapter.
- *Chapter Summary*, at the end of each chapter, serves as a review of the key concepts covered in the chapter.
- *Review Questions* allow the learner to test their comprehension of the chapter content.
- *Hands-On Projects* encourage the learner to apply the knowledge they have gained after finishing the chapter. Files for the *Hands-On Projects* can be found on the Student Resource Center. Note: you will need your access code provided in your book to enter the site. Visit *www.cengage.com/community/eccouncil* for a link to the Student Resource Center.

Student Resource Center

The Student Resource Center contains all the files you need to complete the Hands-On Projects found at the end of the chapters. Access the Student Resource Center with the access code provided in your book. Instructions for logging onto the Student Resource Site are included with the access code. Visit *www.cengage.com/community/ eccouncil* for a link to the Student Resource Center.

Additional Instructor Resources

Free to all instructors who adopt the *Security and Vulnerability Assessment* book for their courses is a complete package of instructor resources. These resources are available from the Course Technology web site, *www.cengage.com/coursetechnology*, by going to the product page for this book in the online catalog, click on the Companion Site on the Faculty side; click on any of the Instructor Resources in the left navigation and login to access the files. Once you accept the license agreement, the selected files will be displayed.

Resources include:

- *Instructor Manual*: This manual includes course objectives and additional information to help your instruction.

- *ExamView Testbank*: This Windows-based testing software helps instructors design and administer tests and pre-tests. In addition to generating tests that can be printed and administered, this full-featured program has an online testing component that allows students to take tests at the computer and have their exams automatically graded.

- *PowerPoint Presentations*: This book comes with a set of Microsoft PowerPoint slides for each chapter. These slides are meant to be used as a teaching aid for classroom presentations, to be made available to students for chapter review, or to be printed for classroom distribution. Instructors are also at liberty to add their own slides.

- *Labs*: Additional Hands-on Activities to provide additional practice for your students.

- *Assessment Activities*: Additional assessment opportunities including discussion questions, writing assignments, internet research activities, and homework assignments along with a final cumulative project.

- *Final Exam*: Provides a comprehensive assessment of *Security and Vulnerability Assessment* content.

Cengage Learning Information Security Community Site

This site was created for learners and instructors to find out about the latest in information security news and technology.
Visit *community.cengage.com/infosec* to:

- Learn what's new in information security through live news feeds, videos and podcasts.

- Connect with your peers and security experts through blogs and forums.

- Browse our online catalog.

How to Become E|NSA Certified

The E|NSA certification ensures that the learner has the fundamental skills needed to analyze the internal and external security threats against a network, and to develop security policies that will protect an organization's information. E|NSA certified individuals will know how to evaluate network and Internet security issues and design, and how to implement successful security policies and firewall strategies as well as how to expose system and network vulnerabilities and defend against them.

E|NSA Certification exams are available through Prometric Prime. To finalize your certification after your training, you must:

1. Purchase an exam voucher from the EC-Council Community Site at Cengage: *www.cengage.com/community/eccouncil*.

2. Speak with your Instructor or Professor about scheduling an exam session, or visit the EC-Council Community Site referenced above for more information.

3. Take and pass the E|NSA certification examination with a score of 70% or better.

About Our Other EC-Council | Press Products

Ethical Hacking and Countermeasures Series

The EC-Council | Press *Ethical Hacking and Countermeasures* series is intended for those studying to become security officers, auditors, security professionals, site administrators, and anyone who is concerned about or responsible for the integrity of the network infrastructure. The series includes a broad base of topics in offensive network security, ethical hacking, as well as network defense and countermeasures. The content of this series is designed to immerse the learner into an interactive environment where they will be shown how to scan, test, hack and secure information systems. A wide variety of tools, viruses, and malware is presented in these books, providing a complete understanding of the tactics and tools used by hackers. By gaining a thorough understanding of how hackers operate, ethical hackers are able to set up strong countermeasures and defensive systems to protect their organization's critical infrastructure and information. The series when used in its entirety helps prepare readers to take and succeed on the C|EH certification exam from EC-Council.

Books in Series:
- *Ethical Hacking and Countermeasures: Attack Phases*/143548360X
- *Ethical Hacking and Countermeasures: Threats and Defense Mechanisms*/1435483618
- *Ethical Hacking and Countermeasures: Web Applications and Data Servers*/1435483626
- *Ethical Hacking and Countermeasures: Linux, Macintosh and Mobile Systems*/1435483642
- *Ethical Hacking and Countermeasures: Secure Network Infrastructures*/1435483650

Computer Forensics Series

The EC-Council | Press *Computer Forensics* series, preparing learners for C|HFI certification, is intended for those studying to become police investigators and other law enforcement personnel, defense and military personnel, e-business security professionals, systems administrators, legal professionals, banking, insurance and other professionals, government agencies, and IT managers. The content of this program is designed to expose the learner to the process of detecting attacks and collecting evidence in a forensically sound manner with the intent to report crime and prevent future attacks. Advanced techniques in computer investigation and analysis with interest in generating potential legal evidence are included. In full, this series prepares the learner to identify evidence in computer related crime and abuse cases as well as track the intrusive hacker's path through client system.

Books in Series:
- *Computer Forensics: Investigation Procedures and Response*/1435483499
- *Computer Forensics: Investigating Hard Disks, File and Operating Systems*/1435483502
- *Computer Forensics: Investigating Data and Image Files*/1435483510
- *Computer Forensics: Investigating Network Intrusions and Cybercrime*/1435483529
- *Computer Forensics: Investigating Wireless Networks and Devices*/1435483537

Penetration Testing Series

The EC-Council | Press *Penetration Testing* series, preparing learners for E|CSA/LPT certification, is intended for those studying to become Network Server Administrators, Firewall Administrators, Security Testers, System Administrators and Risk Assessment professionals. This series covers a broad base of topics in advanced penetration testing and security analysis. The content of this program is designed to expose the learner to groundbreaking methodologies in conducting thorough security analysis, as well as advanced penetration testing techniques. Armed with the knowledge from the Security Analyst series, learners will be able to perform the intensive assessments required to effectively identify and mitigate risks to the security of the organization's infrastructure. The series when used in its entirety helps prepare readers to take and succeed on the E|CSA, Certified Security Analyst certification exam.

E|CSA certification is a relevant milestone towards achieving EC-Council's Licensed Penetration Tester (LPT) designation, which also ingrains the learner in the business aspect of penetration testing. To learn more about this designation please visit http://www.eccouncil.org/lpt.htm.

Books in Series:
- *Penetration Testing: Security Analysis*/1435483669
- *Penetration Testing: Procedures and Methodologies*/1435483677
- *Penetration Testing: Network and Perimeter Testing*/1435483685
- *Penetration Testing: Communication Media Testing*/1435483693
- *Penetration Testing: Network Threat Testing*/1435483707

Cyber Safety/1435483715

Cyber Safety is designed for anyone who is interested in learning computer networking and security basics. This product provides information cyber crime; security procedures; how to recognize security threats and attacks, incident response, and how to secure internet access. This book gives individuals the basic security literacy skills to begin high-end IT programs. The book also prepares readers to take and succeed on the Security|5 certification exam from EC-Council.

Wireless Safety/1435483766

Wireless Safety introduces the learner to the basics of wireless technologies and its practical adaptation. *Wireless|5* is tailored to cater to any individual's desire to learn more about wireless technology. It requires no pre-requisite knowledge and aims to educate the learner in simple applications of these technologies. Topics include wireless signal propagation, IEEE and ETSI Wireless Standards, WLANs and Operation, Wireless Protocols and Communication Languages, Wireless Devices, and Wireless Security Network. The book also prepares readers to take and succeed on the Wireless|5 certification exam from EC-Council.

Network Safety/1435483774

Network Safety provides the basic core knowledge on how infrastructure enables a working environment. Intended for those in an office environment and for the home user who wants to optimize resource utilization, share infrastructure and make the best of technology and the convenience it offers. Topics include foundations of networks, networking components, wireless networks, basic hardware components, the networking environment and connectivity as well as troubleshooting. The book also prepares readers to take and succeed on the Network|5 certification exam from EC-Council.

Disaster Recovery Series

The *Disaster Recovery Series* is designed to fortify virtualization technology knowledge of system administrators, systems engineers, enterprise system architects, and any IT professional who is concerned about the integrity of the their network infrastructure. Virtualization technology gives the advantage of additional flexibility as well as cost savings while deploying a disaster recovery solution. The series when used in its entirety helps prepare readers to take and succeed on the E|CDR and E|CVT, Disaster Recovery and Virtualization Technology certification exam from EC-Council. The EC-Council Certified Disaster Recovery and Virtualization Technology professional will have a better understanding of how to setup Disaster Recovery Plans using traditional and virtual technologies to ensure business continuity in the event of a disaster.

Books in Series
- *Disaster Recovery*/1435488709
- *Virtualization Security*/1435488695

Acknowledgements

Michael H. Goldner is the Chair of the School of Information Technology for ITT Technical Institute in Norfolk Virginia, and also teaches bachelor level courses in computer network and information security systems. Michael has served on and chaired ITT Educational Services Inc. National Curriculum Committee on Information Security. He received his Juris Doctorate from Stetson University College of Law, his undergraduate degree from Miami University and has been working over fifteen years in the area of Information Technology. He is an active member of the American Bar Association, and has served on that organization's Cyber Law committee. He is a member of IEEE, ACM and ISSA, and is the holder of a number of industrially recognized certifications including, CISSP, CEH, CHFI, CEI, MCT, MCSE/Security, Security +, Network + and A+. Michael recently completed the design and creation of a computer forensic program for ITT Technical Institute, and has worked closely with both EC-Council and Delmar/Cengage Learning in the creation of this EC-Council Press series.

Chapter 1

Web Security

Objectives

After completing this chapter, you should be able to:

- Understand the various types of network threats
- Identify unauthorized network devices
- Identify client authorization mechanisms and techniques
- Deploy and manage Web-based solutions
- Understand plug-ins
- Understand Common Gateway Interfaces

Key Terms

E-pending the process of guessing e-mail addresses using specific names

Introduction to Web Security

Because Web sites are increasingly important to commercial business, Web security is of great concern. Web sites are an organization's open link to the outside world, which means they are often the easiest places for an attacker to enter the internal network. This chapter shows you how to secure Web servers, clients, and networks.

Web Architecture

The architecture of the Web includes clients, DNS servers, Web servers, and networks to connect those servers. This relationship is shown in Figure 1-1. All of these must be secured.

The user typically sends a request to the DNS server by typing a URL into the Web browser. The DNS server then translates the requested hostname into the IP address of the desired Web site. Using that IP address, a connection is established and a request is sent to the Web server. The Web server then sends the requested Web page to the user client. The browser displays that Web page.

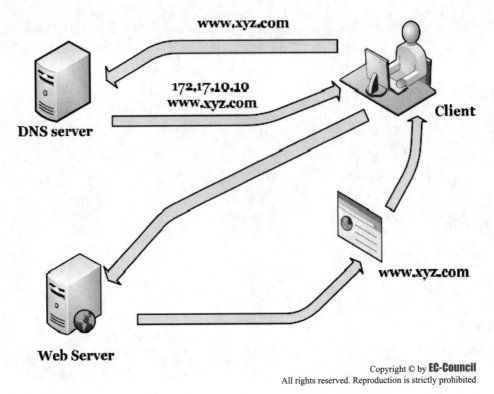

Figure 1-1   The Web includes clients, Web servers, DNS servers, and networks connecting them.

Common Threats on the Web

Web threats can be client side, server side, or on the network.

- Many computers on the client side are vulnerable to attacks like viruses, worms, and Trojans.
- Data available on Web servers are exposed to unauthorized access. If an intrusion occurs on the Web server, it could lead to a reduction in speed or may even crash the server.
- If a network on the Web is not properly secured, information may be intercepted during transfer. These data could then be altered and sent back. Hackers often attack networks that are not sufficiently secured.

Identity Theft

Identity theft is a serious form of criminal fraud, in which someone uses someone else's identity. Identity theft can be used for financial fraud, such as credit card or bank fraud, or could be used to cover up other criminal activities.

Spam

Spam is any commercially driven, unwanted bulk mailing. Spammers have developed a range of spamming techniques, including: e-mail spam, instant messaging spam, Usenet newsgroup spam, Web search engine spam, Web log spam, and mobile messaging spam.

E-mail spam involves transmitting identical, or nearly identical, unwanted messages to a huge number of receivers. Most e-mail programs and servers have filters to detect spam, but modern spammers have created tricks to bypass these filters.

Spammers acquire e-mail addresses through a variety of means, including searching Usenet postings, DNS listings, and Web pages, and guessing common names at familiar domains. One technique, known as *e-pending*, involves guessing e-mail addresses using specific names, such as residents in a community. Many spammers employ programs called Web spiders to harvest e-mail addresses from Web pages. It is, however, possible to deceive these programs by replacing the @ symbol with another symbol, such as # or even the word *at*, when posting an e-mail address.

E-mail spammers are careful to hide the origin of their messages. They can achieve this by spoofing e-mail addresses, which is similar to Internet Protocol spoofing. Spammers alter e-mail messages to make them appear as though they are originating from another address.

Distributed Denial-Of-Service Attack

An attacker can initiate a distributed denial-of-service (DDoS) attack by compromising multiple computers and installing an application on them that simultaneously initiates packet flooding to a target system.

DDoS attacks are easy to perform but can cause a great amount of damage. They can halt systems entirely or allow attackers to gain access. First, the intruder attacks certain systems and halts services to these systems. These systems are known as the primary victims. These victim computers are used to attack other systems, called secondary victims. The primary victims and secondary victims create a network of systems that spread the DDoS attack, which makes it difficult, if not impossible, to identify the ultimate source of the attack.

The following are the three basic types of DDoS attacks:

1. Using large amounts of computational resources such as bandwidth, disk space, or CPU time

2. Corrupting network settings such as routing tables

3. Damaging physical network components

Commonly used DDoS attack tools include the following:

- Trinoo
- Tribe Flood Network (TFN)
- Tribe Flood Network 2000 (TFN2K)

To protect against DDoS attacks, administrators should filter incoming and outgoing packets.

Reflection DDoS Attack

A DDoS attack is actually a collection of many techniques (such as worms, viruses, and SYN flooding), all with the objective of denying legitimate clients access to services running on Internet-based servers. Reflection DoS attacks uses the SYN flooding method. However, instead of sending SYN packets directly to the victim server, these attacks reflect the packets off any router or server connected to the Internet.

A TCP connection between two machines requires the exchange of three Internet packets, known as a TCP three-way handshake. This occurs over the following three steps:

1. A TCP client, such as a Web browser or an FTP client, sends a SYN packet to the server to start the connection.

2. As soon as the server receives the packet on an open TCP service port, the operating system of the server responds with a connection-accepting SYN/ACK packet.

3. After receiving the SYN/ACK packet, the client replies with an ACK packet.

In the reflection attack, the attacking machine sends a large number of SYN packets with a source IP address that points to the target machine. This way, all receiving hosts send SYN/ACK packets to the victim, which overwhelms the victim.

The Internet server is able to reflect SYN packets for any general purpose TCP connection. The following is a short list of popular TCP ports:

- 21 (FTP)
- 22 (Secure Shell)
- 23 (Telnet)
- 25 (SMTP)
- 53 (DNS)
- 80 (HTTP/Web)
- 110 (POP3)

In addition, virtually all routers will accept TCP connections on port 179.

Parasitic Malware

Parasitic malware is a type of virus that modifies existing files on a disk by injecting malicious code. When the user runs an infected file, the virus is injected into the system. Common parasitic files include W32/Bacalid, W32/Polip, and W32/Detnat. These files hide from users and attempt to download Trojans from compromised Web sites.

Bots

A botnet, or zombie army, is a network of computers performing automated tasks. These can be used for positive purposes, like adding information to search engines, or for negative purposes, like DoS attacks.

Systems that are not patched are the most vulnerable to attack from botnets. As the size of a network increases, the possibility of vulnerabilities also increases. An intruder can scan network ranges to identify which computers are the most vulnerable. In order to attack a system, an intruder targets machines with Class B network ranges.

When an attacker compromises a system, an Internet Relay Chat (IRC) bot can be installed, also called a zombie or drone. It connects to a particular IRC channel on an IRC server in order to allow the intruder to manage or monitor the computer.

Cross-Site Request Forgery

Cross-site request forgery (XSRF or CSRF) is a type of Web site attack in which an intruder acts as a trusted user. The attacker can then change firewall settings, post unauthorized data on a forum, or conduct fraudulent financial transactions. Because all changes appear to be performed by an authorized user, it may be difficult to even know that an attack has occurred.

An XSRF attack can be executed by sending an unauthorized HTTP request to a legitimate user and gathering sensitive user data. This is difficult to defend against because as a less common attack it does not receive very much attention. In addition, it can be difficult to determine the origin of an HTTP request. Frequent use of cryptographic tokens can provide authentication for these requests.

Session Hijacking

TCP session hijacking is carried out through source-routed IP packets. A hacker can intercept the conversation of other users by diverting packets to his or her own system. The man-in-the-middle (MITM) attack is another method in which a sniffer is used to intercept a conversation between two users.

Session hijacking involves the following steps:

1. Tracking the connection
2. Desynchronizing the connection
3. Injecting new packets

It is very difficult to identify intrusions, but if the Web site is not properly responding, the session may have been hijacked.

Smurf Attack

A Smurf attack is a network-level attack against hosts. The perpetrator sends a large amount of ICMP echo (ping) traffic to IP broadcast addresses, all having the spoofed source address of a victim. If the routing device delivering traffic to those broadcast addresses accepts the IP broadcast, hosts on that IP network will take the ICMP echo request and reply to the victim. On a multiaccess broadcast network, there could potentially be hundreds of machines replying to each packet, ensuring that the spoofed host may no longer be able to receive or distinguish legitimate traffic.

This attack can be prevented by denying broadcast addresses from Web servers. All routers in the network should be configured to deny IP-directed broadcasts from one network into another and to block IP spoofing. Properly configured routers will block packets that originate from inside the network.

A Fraggle attack is similar to a Smurf attack, except it uses UDP echo packets instead of ICMP echo packets. IRC servers and their providers are the most common targets of these attacks.

FTP Bounce

FTP (File Transfer Protocol) is used to transfer files and data between a host system and a server. In an FTB bounce attack, the attacker will upload a file to an FTP server and request that server send the file into an internal server, bypassing application-based firewalls. This file may contain malicious code or a simple script to take control of the FTP server in order to use the memory and resources of the computer.

This attack can be avoided by regularly updating the FTP daemon on the Web server. FTP sites should be regularly monitored for anonymous files. Firewalls and the Nmap scanning tool will usually detect this attack. Firewalls will filter the contents and commands in the FTP server and also block some file extensions that often contain malicious code. The Nmap port scanner actually uses FTP bounce attacks to scan other servers.

RSS/Atomic Injection

An RSS (Really Simple Syndication) feed is a common platform for sharing information on portals and Web applications. These feeds allow both users and Web sites to gather content headlines and body text without visiting the site in question, providing a summary of that site's content.

JavaScript can be included in RSS feeds to attack the client's browser. During the presentation phase, most RSS readers treat the received data as plaintext and will execute any script contained in the feed. Therefore, it is important to filter out certain characteristics of RSS feeds on the server side.

DNS Attack

Program and design flaws may allow a hacker to poison DNS server information with incorrect data, misdirecting users. A DNS attack is one way to perform a DoS attack.

Content Spoofing

Content spoofing is when hackers create a Web site that looks exactly like a different, trusted site, in order to defraud victims (phishing). This creates a trust relationship between the user and the attacker, which may lead the user to reveal confidential information.

Hackers usually lead users to spoofed content through e-mail, bulletin board postings, and chat room transmissions. In some cases, an attacker can change the information and links in an established and trusted Web site by accessing and altering content on the server.

The most dangerous content spoofing is done with DHTML (dynamic HTML) content sources such as forms and login applications. When an Internet user views a Web page with spoofed content, the location bar displays what appears to be a valid URL. As a result, when the user enters sensitive data (such as a credit card number, password, bank account number, birth date, or Social Security number), the attacker can steal that user's identity.

Logical Attacks

Logical attacks occur when attackers misuse a Web application's logic flow. Some of the best examples of application logic flow are password recovery, account registration, bid auditing, and e-commerce purchases. In general, to complete a particular process, a Web site may need a user to correctly perform a specific multistep process, which an attacker can misuse.

Types of logical attacks include:

- *Functionality abuse*: The functionality and features of a Web site are used to defraud users or avoid access control mechanisms.

- *Insufficient antiautomation*: A Web site permits an attacker to automate a process without human interaction.

- *Insufficient process validation*: A Web site allows an attacker to alter or modify the actual flow control of an application.

Buffer Overflow

A buffer overflow occurs when an application or process attempts to store more data in a buffer than it can hold. A buffer is a part of memory used for the temporary storage of data, including user input and messages received from remote systems. The size of a buffer is restricted. After a buffer's limit is reached, data are redirected to the closest buffer, where they will overwrite whatever data are already inside.

A buffer overflow is an attack on information reliability. During these attacks, the excess data may contain code intended to corrupt the user's files, alter data, or reveal confidential information. This can even occur through an e-mail message header, in which the user does not have to open the message for the attack to be delivered.

IP and Routing Protocol Spoofing

IP spoofing occurs when attackers, from the inside or outside, of a network attempt to gain access to a restricted resource by concealing their systems' IP addresses. IP spoofing can be used to hide the details of an IP address when browsing a Web site, chatting online, sending e-mails, or any other online activity.

In spoofing attacks, malicious routing updates are sent to routers, firewalls, or proxy servers in order to make them reroute packets to a server monitored by an attacker. Later, these packets will be redirected to the correct destination. This problem can be lessened by protecting the routing update packets using the following:

- Plaintext passwords
- Cryptographic checksums
- Encryption

Identifying Unauthorized Network Devices

For small networks, it is relatively easy to keep track of the physical location of each network device in use, but it is more difficult in large networks with dozens, or even hundreds, of devices. A device inventory ensures that the router that connects the Web site to the ISP is safe. Still, the devices in the inventory can be rearranged, so they must be checked and verified in order to match hostnames in the inventory. The physical inventory lists all the devices that are permitted on the network. It also covers additional devices available in a restricted area like the server room.

IP address sweeping detects redundant network devices in each network segment. The best way to do this is to ping with ICMP (Internet Control Message Protocol). The following is the syntax of ping, where *xxx.xxx.xxx.xxx* is the internal IP address of the device:

```
ping xxx.xxx.xxx.xxx
```

A ping sweep is defined as detecting active IP addresses on a specified network segment. If the administrator configures one or more devices to not respond to a ping, the sweep must be performed with another network protocol like TCP or UDP. The sweeps consume more time when they scan all the network addresses manually, so various automated tools can be used.

An IP address sweep can be seen as a sign of an attacker sniffing in the vicinity. The testing team must ensure that the IP sweeps are not mistaken for actual attacks.

Restrictive Access

Users must only be allowed to use valid and necessary applications. These restrictions are in place to ensure that unauthorized users, should they gain access, may not use too many applications. Types of user restrictions include functional restrictions, data restrictions, and cross-related restrictions, and they must all be tested to ensure that the proper permissions are granted.

Functional Restrictions

Users can be granted or denied access to specific functional capabilities of an application. For instance, a registered user who logs into a stock-trading application might have a time delay in receiving information, while stockbrokers would have no delay.

The decisions the Web designer makes must be based on the necessary and unnecessary functions required by each user and whether they should be displayed on the Web applications. In general, inaccessible options should not be presented in the user interface, because it complicates the learning process.

Data Restrictions

Web application designers can restrict access to sensitive data so that users cannot modify or view it.

Cross-Related Restrictions

These are a combination of both functional and data restrictions. They restrict data access indirectly by denying users access to application functionality. Applications can be directly blocked when unauthorized data are accessed.

Network Addresses

Various techniques can be used to check each network device in order to be sure it uses the network address given to it by the device inventory (the DHCP server). Some commercial network auditing and management tools, such as GFI LANguard, generate reports documenting the configured network addresses. Tools such as LANguard allow the network administrator to not only scan the network and confirm correctly assigned IP addresses, but to detect, assess, and correct any potential security risk to the network.

Altering the Network Address

When data packets are transmitted from one machine to another, the sender must ensure that the network address can be converted from one format to the other. During transmission, the translations available in the cache are refreshed frequently. Attackers can damage this mapping and redirect or mislead the traffic to other devices. These cases are minimized by setting network address translation to static.

DNS Cache Poisoning

All DNS servers include a cache of recently queried IP addresses to domain name links. They also contain records of authorized devices such as the mail server (Mx) or the Active Directory domain controller (Srv). The cache manages and maintains data for a set period of time. An intruder can inject a false IP address and link it to a specific domain name, such as Google. When the user tries to go to the Google Web site, he or she is sent instead to the attacker's spoofed Web site, where information may be harvested and stolen.

Routing Table Poisoning

Routing table poisoning is when the attacker misleads traffic by altering the routing table. These tables are used by devices to send traffic to the correct destination device. Periodic manual testing will determine if the router is properly configured.

ARP Spoofing

In this technique, also known as a man-in-middle (MITM) attack, a third party listens to communications between two parties. This allows the computer to discover the MAC address of any other unknown computer. ARP can convert IP addresses to physical network addresses (MAC addresses). Attackers use tools like Arpwatch and Etttercap to accomplish ARP spoofing.

Tracking Connectivity

In small networks, network connectivity can be checked with a simple visual inspection. More complicated networks may need to be checked with built-in commands, like tracert in Windows or traceroute in UNIX. These commands determine the path used by an ICMP request from the source to the destination. Figure 1-2 shows the results of a Windows tracert command.

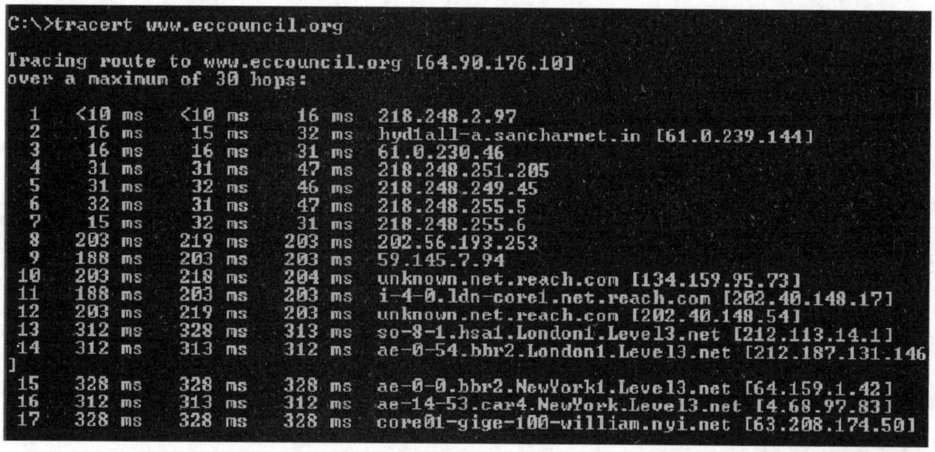

```
C:\>tracert www.eccouncil.org

Tracing route to www.eccouncil.org [64.90.176.10]
over a maximum of 30 hops:

  1    <10 ms    <10 ms     16 ms   218.248.2.97
  2     16 ms     15 ms     32 ms   hyd1all-a.sancharnet.in [61.0.239.144]
  3     16 ms     16 ms     31 ms   61.0.230.46
  4     31 ms     31 ms     47 ms   218.248.251.205
  5     31 ms     32 ms     46 ms   218.248.249.45
  6     32 ms     31 ms     47 ms   218.248.255.5
  7     15 ms     32 ms     31 ms   218.248.255.6
  8    203 ms    219 ms    203 ms   202.56.193.253
  9    188 ms    203 ms    203 ms   59.145.7.94
 10    203 ms    218 ms    204 ms   unknown.net.reach.com [134.159.95.73]
 11    188 ms    203 ms    203 ms   i-4-0.ldn-core1.net.reach.com [202.40.148.17]
 12    203 ms    219 ms    203 ms   unknown.net.reach.com [202.40.148.54]
 13    312 ms    328 ms    313 ms   so-8-1.hsa1.London1.Level3.net [212.113.14.1]
 14    312 ms    313 ms    312 ms   ae-0-54.bbr2.London1.Level3.net [212.187.131.146
]
 15    328 ms    328 ms    328 ms   ae-0-0.bbr2.NewYork1.Level3.net [64.159.1.42]
 16    312 ms    313 ms    312 ms   ae-14-53.car4.NewYork.Level3.net [4.68.97.83]
 17    328 ms    328 ms    328 ms   core01-gige-100-william.nyi.net [63.208.174.50]
```

Figure 1-2   The Windows tracert utility shows the path an IMCP packet takes to go from the source to the destination.

Testing Traffic-Filtering Devices

Testing filtering devices is necessary to ensure that authorized traffic passes through the filters unregulated. With multiple filters, such as DMZ configuration, each filter must be tested to guarantee that it has been appropriately configured. This requires changing the source address with respect to inbound and outbound tests.

Firewalls can be configured to log inbound and outbound requests. This can be valuable evidence in legal proceedings. Endurance tests ensure that logging over long periods of time does not interfere with a firewall's normal operation. When the load is increased on the device, it becomes more difficult for the firewall to determine what is to be filtered and what is not, so stress testing is important.

Installing and Protecting IIS

Internet Information Services (IIS) can be easily installed on a Windows system. IIS contains several optional components that should be installed. To install IIS in Windows, add optional components, or remove optional components, an administrator should follow these steps:

1. Enter the Windows Control Panel, and open **Add or Remove Programs**.

2. Click **Add or Remove Components**.

3. Follow the instructions to install, remove, or add components to IIS.

IIS has built-in virtual directory security. This security provides permission for reading, writing, and executing scripts stored within a virtual directory. These permissions are independent of file-system permissions. The following are available security rights in the virtual directory:

- *Script source access* allows users to view the source code of applications within the directory.

- *Read access privilege* allows users to view or download the files from the directory.

- *Write access privilege* allows users to upload files to the directory.

- *Directory browsing* allows users to view an HTML page with a list of the files in the directory.

Client Authorization

Users must authenticate themselves to obtain access to some Web applications. This is unnecessary for most Web applications. However, when sensitive data are involved, it is crucial. User authentication in Web applications can be done with one of these techniques:

- User-created passwords

- Personal property of the user, such as keys

- Unique physical features, like fingerprints or retina scans

These techniques are applied in different ways, depending on the required cost, usage, and accuracy. Accuracy can be calculated in terms of the following:

- The percentage of users who should be authorized but are not; called the false-rejection rate

- The percentage of unauthorized users who can deceive the system into believing they should be authorized; known as the false-acceptance rate

Certificate Authorities

Certificate authorities (CAs) provide public keys for message encryption and also manage the security issues in the network. In public-key infrastructure (PKI), a CA along with a registration authority (RA), checks the information provided by the requestor of a digital certificate. If the RA verifies that information, then the CA can issue a digital certificate.

Client-Side Data

In some situations, sensitive information like user IDs, passwords, credit card numbers, and Social Security numbers can accumulate on the user's hard drive in unencrypted form. This allows intruders to view, analyze, and modify this information with relative ease. This information should be encrypted, which may take more bandwidth than unencrypted data.

Cookies

Cookies are small text files that store data regarding session ID, current time and date, and IP address. These files are sent from a Web browser and are stored on the user's local machine. There are two types of cookies:

1. *Persistent cookies* stay on the machine even when the browser is closed and the computer is turned off. These accumulate on the hard drive. Parity checks minimize cookie poisoning by restricting inconsistent cookies with the parity tag.

2. *Session cookies* are present in browser memory and remain as long as the browser is open. If sufficient memory is not available on the client's machine, session cookies may be stored on the local hard drive.

Hidden Files

Hidden files are substitutes for cookies and can be used if cookies are disabled on the browser. They accumulate the data on the client's computer and can be altered through built-in tools.

URLs

Web applications sometimes insert user IDs and passwords into the URL as an element in the query. This makes the data very easy to observe and corrupt.

Local Data Files

The client may only allow access if temporary or permanent data files are on the system when execution takes place.

Windows Registry

Scripts such as ActiveX controls sometimes use the client's Windows registry for data storage. Regedit, a built-in Windows utility, can be used to view registry data.

Server-Side Data

Confidential information should not be stored in files with readable file-names. This makes it easy for intruders to locate and steal or corrupt the information. Server-side security measures can be taken to overcome this threat, including:

- Data filenames
- Data tripwires
- Data vaults
- WORMs
- Data encryption
- Data deception
- Data islands
- Distributed copies
- Fragmented data

Data Filenames

If information on user accounts, such as the usernames and passwords, has to be stored on the Web server, administrators should never use descriptive filenames such as username or password. The filenames should not be so obscure as to cause confusion, but they should not be extremely obvious, in order to avoid inviting attacks.

Data Tripwires

If passwords and usernames are stored in obscurely named files, obviously named files can also be included. If these files are accessed, an alarm can warn the security administrator of potential unauthorized access.

Data Vaults

Data can be placed in a data repository called a data vault for additional security. The testing team should ensure that all data are properly stored in these data vaults.

WORMs

Using WORM (write once, read many) devices, such as CD-Rs and DVD-Rs, makes it impossible for intruders to remotely modify system logs.

Data Encryption

Files containing Web logs, database logs, .ini files, and others need to be encrypted so that no matter where they are stored, they are secure.

Data Deception

Data deception uses heavy encryption algorithms to display encrypted data as if it were not encrypted.

Data Islands

After uploading the master database to the Web application, connections between the Web application and the physical system are disconnected. This prevents intruders from accessing the actual storage. It should be tested to ensure the link is indeed severed.

Distributed Copies

To enhance scalability, some Web sites distribute data to servers spread across the network in different locations. This would make it necessary for an intruder to gain access to all locations in order to obtain the data. Access to these servers should be tested to ensure that no more than one copy of the data can be accessed.

Fragmented Data

Breaking the data into multiple pieces and distributing it across multiple servers prevents intruders from accessing the complete data. If this is used, it is important that the developer does not reassemble the data into a temporary file that, if found by an intruder, provides the entire file.

User Approaches

There are two possible user approaches: the "know something" approach and the "has something" approach. With the "know something" approach, the user can be identified using personal information like a username and password. If there are any problems with authentication, the user can be asked a secret question such as, "What was the name of the first school you attended?"

Using the "has something" approach, the user is authenticated using physical tokens, such as smart cards, software-related personal certificates, or the IP address of a network device. This approach must be carefully tested before it is put into operation.

Authentication Techniques

In addition to standard usernames and passwords, some authentication techniques include:

- Personal certificates
- Smart cards
- MAC addresses
- IP addresses
- Telephone numbers

Personal Certificates

A personal certificate is a small data file authorized by a certification authority (CA). The encrypted ID in the data file enables the CA owner to transfer encrypted and digitally signed information through the network. This assures the recipient that the information sent is not forged or corrupted.

Personal certificates are generally a stronger form of user authentication than are usernames and passwords. These certificates are kept away from the public.

Smart Cards

A secure ID smart card uses encryption mechanisms for creating new passwords every minute to increase the efficiency of the user authentication. In addition to possessing the physical card, the user must provide a memorized PIN to ensure that the card was not stolen.

MAC Address

Web servers can determine the MAC address of any client connecting to the Web site. Commands like ifconfig (for UNIX/Linux) and **ipconfig /all** (for Windows) display the NIC MAC addresses. This address can be used for authorization; however, it should be noted that MAC spoofing is a very simple task.

IP Addresses

Data packets contain specific source IP addresses that can be used to identify the sender. This should not be considered secure, as proxy servers can conceal the IP addresses and the source IP addresses in the data packets can be easily modified.

Telephone Numbers

Many organizations, such as credit card companies, use the telephone numbers of their customers to authenticate them.

Input Data Validation

A Web application can receive input data in a number of ways. Because the attacker could alter or disable any client-side authentication routine, none of the input data should be processed until a server-side authentication mechanism checks it.

Invalid Data Types

Many programming languages do not receive input data properly from the program's input fields. This can lead to data truncation, inappropriate communications, and even the destruction of the program itself. If invalid data are not captured by the data validation function, the receiving application may malfunction. Every data validation function must be tested to guarantee that it is able to properly manage input data of the incorrect data types. This testing can be done by editing the HTML used to create the data input Web page, giving a custom test connection, or using the scripting functionalities of a functional testing tool.

Invalid Ranges

A Web developer can consider certain incorporated validation functionalities of a client-side language to guarantee that an input value is not longer than intended. For instance, JavaScript can be used to guarantee that when the user is asked to input a month, the value will be between 1 and 12. Scripting tools can be used to enter several combinations of test inputs. Two customary testing techniques, called equivalence partitioning and boundary value analysis, are used for detecting the best test data for invalid-range testing.

Deploying and Managing Web-Based Solutions

Browsing Analysis

Web browser analysis includes:

- *Analyzing HTTP headers*: The information contained in the HTTP header displays the most recently browsed Web page of the client, which determines if the page logged in is a valid navigational request.

This header information can be modified through the HTTP-EQUIV metatags Cache control, Expires, and Pragma.

- *Checking client-side scripting*: Certain applications depend on the application code to restrict access to confidential data. Client-side scripts are used to enter user details. Before using this technique, it must be tested for scripting, Java applets, or ActiveX.

- *Using session IDs*: A Web application can identify the user's browser and use a session ID to check the user's privileges and permissions.

- *Using link checking tools*: A large number of Web pages must be tested with different privileges. Test scripts should be established using link checking tools.

Browser Security

A Web browser is one of the most important Web applications. Most Web browsers have significant security flaws, making users vulnerable to attackers if they visit Web sites with malicious content. Visit the following Web site for information on securing specific Web browsers:

http://www.us-cert.gov/reading_room/securing_browser/

It is important to address the following settings:

- Cookies
- Encryption capabilities
- Client-side mobile code (applets)
- Tiny windows, in which TCP receive windows are kept small to defend against malware being injected
- Multiple domains and redirection
- Automatic updates

Browser Hijacking

Browser hijacking is a type of online attack in which hackers take control of a Web browser and change the way it displays information. It can be prevented by keeping the computer updated with the latest security updates and antivirus software. Indicators of browser hijacking include the following:

- The home page settings have been changed
- Web pages for security sites fail to load
- The entire screen fills with ads and pop-ups
- New toolbars or favorites are installed on the computer
- The computer runs slowly

If Internet Explorer has been hijacked, the user should end the iexplore.exe process from the Windows Task Manager and run antivirus software. The hijack attempt may have changed Internet Explorer settings, so he or she should be sure to change them back and restart the computer.

The Stinger, CWShredder, and Windows Defender tools help to stop browser hijacking.

McAfee Stinger

Stinger is a standalone utility used to detect and remove certain viruses in browser-hijacked systems. While it is not a full virus protection tool, it provides a quick and easy way to clean an infected system. Stinger uses advanced scanning technologies including process scanning, digitally signed DAT files, and scan performance optimizations.

Figure 1-3 shows the Stinger tool.

CWShredder

CWShredder is a small utility tool used to remove CoolWebSearch (also CoolWwwSearch, YouFindAll, White-Pages.ws, and others). This tool will scan entire systems to look for this particular hijack. CWShredder is shown in Figure 1-4.

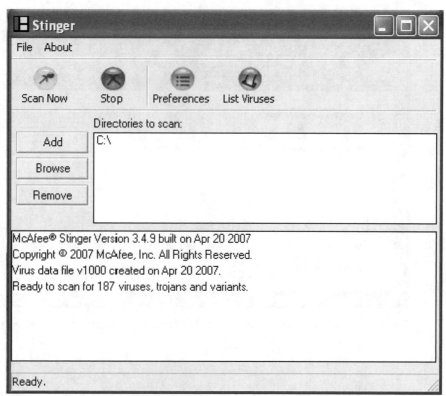

Source: http://vil.nai.com/vil/stinger/. Accessed 2007.

Figure 1-3 The McAfee Stinger tool is a lightweight tool for cleaning an infected system.

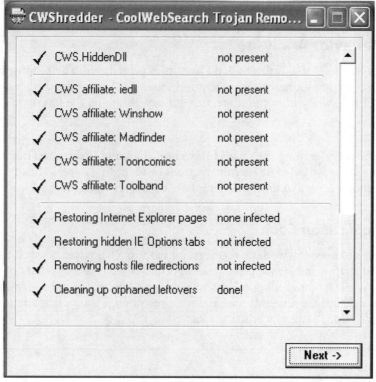

Source: http://www.mac-net.com/1354086.page. Accessed 2004.

Figure 1-4 CWShredder is a tool specifically made to remove CoolWebSearch.

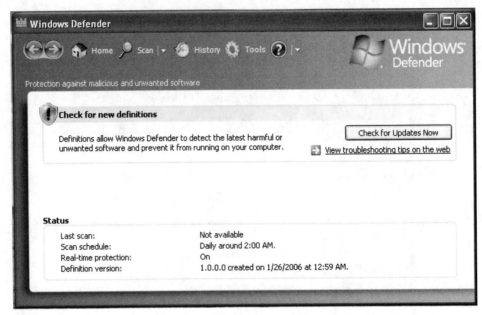

Figure 1-5   Windows Defender protects Windows from unwanted software.

Windows Defender

Windows Defender protects Windows from spyware and other potentially unwanted software. It provides continuous protection using extensive spyware-signature databases, real-time security agents, and an innovative neighborhood watch system. Windows Defender is available from Windows Update and is shown in Figure 1-5.

Browser Behavior Analysis

In order to make sure that a Web site is playing its expected role, an administrator needs to analyze browser behavior. This is a complex activity that requires extensive knowledge and training. It is important to understand consumer behavior within the context of a live Web site on the Internet.

Dynamic Code

Dynamic code is programming code used to dynamically build Web pages. It is specifically used for Web pages whose structure will vary based on user interactions or according to periodically changing content. When a Web server gets a request for a dynamic code template, the server constructs a Web page that is sent to the requesting client.

Securing Application Code

Developers can unknowingly include confidential data in Web pages, as well as server-side programs such as CGI scripts, SSI scripts, and Java applets. It is important to never assume that only the Web administrator would view the code. While it is always a good idea to comment source code, those comments should be removed before the code is uploaded to the server. If they are not, they provide a simple roadmap for an intruder to modify the code. This can be done manually or using tools.

Plug-Ins

A plug-in is a software program that interacts with host applications, like a Web browser or an e-mail program, to perform certain functions. For instance, while modern Web browsers have the ability to listen to audio files and watch videos by default, some Web pages require plug-ins to be installed for these purposes.

Adobe Shockwave and Flash

Adobe's Shockwave and Flash players are the most commonly installed Web browser plug-ins. These players play multimedia applications and interactive Web content such as games, business presentations, entertainment, and advertisements from inside a Web browser.

Apple QuickTime

The QuickTime plug-in plays common video and audio file formats inside Web pages. It is embedded with JavaScript functions to put video on a Web page. It can be used to handle video, sound, animation, graphics, text, music, and even virtual reality scenes inside a Web browser.

QuickTime is available for all major browsers on Windows and Macintosh. UNIX users should use the Xanim plug-in for the same purposes.

Java

The Java plug-in from Sun Microsystems allows Web project managers to direct Java applets and JavaBeans components on Web pages to run using Sun's Java Runtime Environment (JRE). Previously, most browsers had Java built in by default, but newer browsers require users to install it manually.

Java can be enabled in Internet Explorer by following these steps:

1. From the **Tools** menu, click **Internet Options**, and then select the **Advanced** tab.
2. In the list of features that is displayed, check the check boxes next to **Java Console Enabled**, **Java JIT Compiler Enabled**, and **Java Logging Enabled**.
3. Click the **OK** button.
4. Select the **Privacy** tab.
5. Choose a setting of **medium** to allow cookies from third-party Web sites. This setting will not allow these sites to use private information without obtaining permission first.

Mozilla Firefox Extensions

Firefox extensions provide new functionalities to Firefox, which could be anything from a toolbar button to a completely new feature. Extensions customize Firefox to fit the needs of the individual user.

HTML Validator

HTML Validator is a Firefox extension that displays the number of errors on an HTML page in the form of an icon in the status bar when browsing. The details of the errors can then be seen when looking at the HTML source of the page.

Adobe Reader

Formerly known as the Acrobat Reader, the Adobe Reader displays PDF (Portable Document Format) files inside a Web browser.

Windows Media Player

This is a default player for the Windows operating system. Like QuickTime, it can be used to play streaming video, audio, animations, and multimedia presentations on the Web.

Validate Sites HTML

The Validate Sites HTML plug-in allows users to validate the markup of an entire Web site, starting with the browser's current page, using the WDG HTML Validator tool. This plug-in can be started either by right-clicking on the page and selecting **Validate Sites HTML** from the Context menu, or by highlighting a URL, right-clicking it, and selecting **Validate Sites HTML**.

Validate P3P

This plug-in allows the user to validate the P3P policy markup of the browser's current page using the W3C Validator service. It can be called either by right-clicking on the page and selecting **Validate P3P** from the Context menu, or by highlighting a URL contained in plaintext, right-clicking it, and then selecting **Validate P3P**.

View-In

View-in plug-ins are used to view a Web site in Internet Explorer from another browser. This is useful when developing a Web site to make sure it works on as many different browsers as possible. Once this plug-in is installed, right-clicking a link will include an **Open link target in IE** menu item. In addition, right-clicking in the main body of a page will include a **View this page in IE** option.

BugMeNot

BugMeNot improves user privacy by providing usernames and passwords for Web sites that require registration. This bypasses mandatory registration and collection of personal information.

Webpage Speed Report

The Webpage Speed Report plug-in allows the user to send either the current Web page or a highlighted URL to the Web Page Analyzer, an online service provided by WebSiteOptimization.com, which will check the given page and report on its download profile. This provides information including how long the page takes to download, what objects are used in the page, and how they affect its download profile.

This plug-in can be used by right-clicking on the page and selecting **Speed Report** from the context menu, or by highlighting a URL, right-clicking it, and then selecting **Speed Report**. The plug-in will then open a new window and display the report.

Validate Links (W3C)

This plug-in will allow a user to check all links on the specified page that are pointing to valid resources. It can be invoked by right-clicking the page and selecting the **validate_W3Clinks** option from the context menu or by highlighting a URL, right-clicking it, and then selecting **validate_W3clinks**. This plug-in will then open a window and display the validation results.

Open Text

Online forums, mail archives, and other sites include URLs in plaintext. This plug-in allows those URLs to be clicked and followed.

Validate RSS

This plug-in allows users to check the validity of an RSS feed using the RSS Validator service. This plug-in can be invoked by right-clicking on the page and selecting **validate_rss** from the context menu or by right-clicking the plaintext and selecting **validate_rss**. The validation result is then displayed in a new window.

Validate CSS

The Validate CSS plug-in allows users to validate the CSS markup of the browser's current page using the W3C Validator service. This service can be invoked by right-clicking on the page and selecting **validate_css** from the context menu, or by highlighting a URL, right-clicking it, and then selecting **validate_css** from the menu. The validation result is then displayed in a new window.

Common Gateway Interface (CGI)

The Common Gateway Interface (CGI) is a standard interface used to retrieve external programs from information servers. It is similar to HTTP or Web servers, except that CGI programs can retrieve both static and dynamic information.

Because CGI scripts are executables, they can be written in any programming language, which means the client is vulnerable to fake scripts. Therefore, certain security measures should be taken, such as placing CGI applications in a separate directory controlled by the Web master.

A CGI application can be developed in the following languages:

- C/C++
- FORTRAN
- Perl

- TCL
- Any UNIX shell
- Visual Basic
- AppleScript

CGI Script

CGI scripts usually reside in the cgi-bin directory, while the source code for CGI written in nonscripting programming languages resides in the cgi-src directory. It is usually easier to execute CGI scripts than CGI programs, because scripts can be more easily debugged, changed, and managed. The server executes a request for a URL from the client and then directly sends the output in real time as a reply to the client.

For most Web servers, CGI mechanisms are standardized. In the server's root directory, the user creates a subdirectory called cgi-bin. If any file is requested from this directory, the server executes the file rather than simply reading it. The output of the executed program is then sent to the requesting client's Web browser. The executable can be a standard .exe file, like the output of a C compiler, or a Perl script. Perl is the most commonly used language for CGI scripting.

Mechanisms and Variables

CGI employs environment variables to send arguments to an application. The two main environment variables employed are QUERY_STRING and PATH_INFO.

QUERY_STRING

A QUERY_STRING is anything that goes after the question mark (?) within the URL. This information can be appended through an ISINDEX document, or through an HTML document using the GET action. It might also be physically embedded in an HTML anchor tag referring to the client's gateway. This string is typically an information query, such as a search string or the encoded outcome of a GET form.

The string is set in the standard URL format, which changes spaces to + and encodes special symbols using a %xx hexadecimal encoding. It must be decoded in order to be used.

In case the client's gateway fails to decode the outcome from a FORM, the query string is decoded to the command line. For example, the query string "change character" might be given to the application using argv[1]="change" and argv[2]= "character". If this method is employed, no processing of the data is required prior to using the data.

PATH_INFO

CGI permits additional information to be embedded in the URL on the client's gateway, which can be employed to send additional, context-specific data to the scripts. This data is generally made accessible as extra data following the path of the client's gateway in the URL and not encoded with the server.

The best example of PATH_INFO is sending a file location to the CGI application. Consider a CGI program called /cgi-bin/spaces, which is able to process files stored in the server's root directory. By taking account of path information appended to the ending of the URL, spaces knows the location of the document with respect to the root through the PATH_INFO environment variable, or the definite path to the document through the PATH_TRANSLATED environment variable generated by the server.

Third-Party CGI Scripts

Applications that are offered by third parties, including server vendors, often contain security flaws. One example for this is the PHF script, which was a GUI standard script that did not properly parse user input. The attackers who discovered this flaw attached a tag to the operating system command with the phf.cgi script that replies to a request with the contents of the password file. Phfscan is one tool that scans the operating system using the PHF script to discover the password file contents.

CGI scanners can identify many malicious CGI programs and CGI programs with security holes. Every Web server should be scanned with a CGI scanner to ensure that no extra CGI applications were accidentally installed. It should be noted, however, that the HTTP 404 page can be considered by the CGI scanner to be a flawed CGI application, which can make the tool return a false positive.

Server Side Includes (SSIs)

Server Side Includes (SSIs) are markers present in an HTML document. The Web server will dynamically substitute that marker with information just before transporting the requested page to the browser. After viewing the HTML source, it is sometimes impossible to determine if the HTML was fixed or dynamically created. HTML source code files hosting SSI commands are generally saved with the .shtml suffix rather than the original .html suffix to guarantee that the Web server parses the HTML code with an SSI evaluator. Different Web servers execute SSI differently.

The include command can be helpful to a developer who wants to reuse standard elements in multiple Web pages. Common code can be automatically included in the requested Web page at the place indicated by the include statement. The primary threat with this statement is that an attacker can sometimes change a Web page and make it include a normally inaccessible file. Another threat is when executable code is inserted inside a file that will be included in another file. An attacker could download the original code for an included file by directly inputting its URL in a browser, and then the file is downloaded without the original code with the SSI evaluator.

The exec command has even more concerns. This command executes CGI programs or any authentic shell command. If the SSI exec command functionality is activated on a Web browser, the attacker need only figure out a way to fool the Web server into running a malicious command. This can be done in two ways:

1. Uploading an .shtml Web page hosting the susceptible exec command to the Web server and then sending a request through a Web browser

2. Using an SSI command on an authentic Web page

CGI Operation

The operation of CGI in sending data from client to server has the following characteristics:

- Information is sent in the form of a name and value pair.
- Each pair begins with an ampersand (&) sign.
- The pair is separated by an equals (=) sign between the name and the value.
- Information is URL encoded.

URL encoding changes some characters to placeholders and substitutes a hexadecimal ASCII value for some characters. To process the data, this sequence is followed:

1. Get the data from the proper variable depending on whether the POST or GET method was used.

2. Change any placeholders to their correct values (for example, change any plus (+) signs to spaces).

3. Split each group of name value pairs into an array of strings.

4. Convert hexadecimal values back to ASCII character equivalents.

5. Evaluate the respective names and values.

Responding to the Client

Any output to be returned to the client Web browser can be sent to the standard output of the CGI program, as in the following line:

```
print "Content-type: text/html", "\n\n<P>This will appear on the
clients' Web browser.</P> "; # MIME header.
```

Two blank lines must be placed after the parsed header.

The CGI application should send the parsed header to its standard output intercepted by the Web server. From that header, the Web server will then create the required nonparsed HTTP response header to be sent to the client. The parsed header must contain a server directive that may include one or more of the following:

- *Content-type*: Indicates the type of the MIME data being sent back to the client
- *Location*: The URL to which the client Web browser should be directed
- *Status*: An HTTP status code, such as 200 (OK) or 404 (not found)

The CGI application may also send an HTTP response header. The server then creates a nonparsed header from CGI parsed information and sends that header to the client. The following is a valid nonparsed header:

```
HTTP/1.0 200 OK
Server: Netscape-Communications/3.0
Content-type: text/html
```

Using the Client to Call a CGI Application

A client can call a CGI application using one of the following methods:

- When a user press a FORM submit button in an HTML form, the action attribute tag can specify a CGI application. To send data through the Web server, GET and POST methods can be used and data will be sent as part of standard input or as a QUERY_STRING.

- Server-side includes (SSI) can be included in an HTML page, as follows:

```
<!--#exec cgi="/cgi-bin/hits.pl"-->
```

- An HTML IMG tag can be used to call the CGI application as follows:

```
<IMG SRC="/cgi-bin/image">
```

- Client-side script programs can be embedded into an HTML page. For example, JavaScript can be used to call a CGI application program.

Chapter Summary

- The architecture of the Web includes clients, DNS servers, Web servers, and networks to connect those servers.
- Web threats can be client side, server side, or on the network.
- An attacker can initiate a distributed denial-of-service (DDoS) attack by compromising multiple computers and installing an application on them that simultaneously initiates packet flooding to a target system.
- Cross-site request forgery (XSRF or CSRF) is a type of Web site attack in which an intruder acts as a trusted user.
- Users must authenticate themselves to obtain access to some Web applications; this is unnecessary for most Web applications, but when sensitive data are involved, it is crucial.
- Because an attacker could alter or disable any client-side authentication routine, no input data should be processed until a server-side authentication mechanism checks it.
- A plug-in is a software program that interacts with host applications like a Web browser or an e-mail program to perform certain functions such as multimedia file viewing.
- The Common Gateway Interface (CGI) is a standard interface used to retrieve external programs from information servers.

Review Questions

1. What is Web security?

   _____

   _____

   _____

   _____

2. What are some common Web security threats?

   _____

   _____

   _____

   _____

3. What is identity theft?

   _____

   _____

   _____

   _____

4. What is a Smurf attack?

   _____

   _____

   _____

   _____

5. What is an FTP bounce attack?

   _____

   _____

   _____

6. What are some methods to identify unauthorized devices?

   _____

   _____

   _____

7. How can connectivity be tracked using tracert/traceroute?

   _____

   _____

   _____

   _____

8. How are traffic-filtering devices tested?

   _____

   _____

   _____

   _____

9. How is IIS installed?

   _____

   _____

   _____

   _____

10. What is client authorization?

    _____

    _____

    _____

    _____

11. What is a certificate authority?

    _____

    _____

    _____

    _____

12. What are some techniques used in client authorization?

    _____

    _____

    _____

    _____

13. What is input data validation?

    _____

    _____

    _____

    _____

14. What is a plug-in?

    _____

    _____

    _____

    _____

15. What is CGI?

_____

_____

_____

_____

16. What is a CGI script?

_____

_____

_____

_____

17. What are Server Side Includes?

_____

_____

_____

_____

Hands-On Projects

1. Use HTTP Analysis Tools to test a Web site or application for IIS security, performance, and user experience.

   ■ Go to the following Web site: _http://www.port80software.com/support/p80tools.asp_.

   ■ Type the URL in the compression check text box and click the **CHECK** button to test the compression features of the Web site.

   ■ Next, check for cache control by typing the URL in the cache check text box and clicking the **CHECK** button.

   ■ Check whether the HTTP header is divulging the technology platform by typing the URL in the header check text box and clicking the **CHECK** button.

   ■ Finally, check whether the Web site's error pages are customized and user friendly by entering the URL in the error check text box and clicking the **CHECK** button.

2. Use HTML Toolbox to test and repair HTML code, as well as check spelling, browser compatibility, load time, and broken links.

   ■ Go to the following Web site: _http://www.netmechanic.com/products/HTML_Toolbox_FreeSample.shtml_.

   ■ Type the URL and number of pages to be checked and click **Test Now**.

   ■ View feature reports by clicking **Detailed Report**.

3. Use Link Checker to read a Web page, extract the links from it, and test the status of each one.

   ■ Go to the following Web site: _http://www.webmaster-toolkit.com/link-checker.shtml_.

   ■ Type a URL, select the link type, and click **Check Links**.

4. Use Domain Age Tool to determine the approximate age of a Web site and to view how the site looked when it was first created.

   ■ Go to the following Web site: _http://www.cumbrowski.com/CarstenC/Internettechtools.asp_.

   ■ Type the domain name and click **Submit**.

5. Use the Stinger tool to scan specific drives and directories.

   ■ Navigate to Chapter 1 of the Student Resource Center.

   ■ Install and launch the Stinger program.

   ■ Click **Preferences,** select the necessary options, and click **OK.**

   ■ Click **Add,** select the drive or directory to be scanned, and click **OK.**

   ■ Click **Scan Now.**

6. Use the CWShredder tool to find and destroy the CoolWebSearch (CWS) browser hijacker.

   ■ Navigate to Chapter 1 of the Student Resource Center.

   ■ Install and launch the CWShredder program.

   ■ Click **Scan Only.**

Chapter 2

E-Mail Security

Objectives

After completing this chapter, you should be able to:

- Analyze the key concepts of e-mail
- Understand the components of an e-mail
- Configure and test e-mail servers
- Analyze the core elements in e-mail encryption
- Install WorkgroupMail and configure Outlook Express
- Identify common e-mail protocols
- Identify a client-server architecture
- Analyze the risks related to e-mail security
- Use tools to secure e-mail
- Track an e-mail

Key Terms

Attachments   files attached to e-mail messages

Introduction to E-Mail Security

E-mail, short for *electronic mail*, is the most common form of person-to-person communication over the Internet. While most e-mail messages are just plaintext, they can be encoded in HTML, which allows the sender to include pictures, links, and anything else found on a standard Web page. In addition, files can be exchanged quickly and easily as *attachments* to e-mail messages. E-mail reaches its destination, anywhere in the world, within a few minutes or even seconds and is incredibly cost effective. On the other hand, e-mail privacy cannot be ensured, and e-mail provides a common entry point for malicious software. This chapter familiarizes you with e-mail and teaches you how to send and receive e-mails safely and securely.

Elements of E-Mail

The most important elements of e-mail are the following:

- *Mail user agent (MUA)*: An MUA is a client program capable of sending and receiving mail from different users. It uses a word processor to send and receive mail. Popular MUAs include Microsoft Outlook and Mozilla Thunderbird.

- *Mail transfer agent (MTA)*: An MTA is a server program that initiates the transfer of mail from one machine to another. It interfaces with the MDA to send and receive mail.

- *Mail delivery agent (MDA)*: An MDA transfers the mail from one MTA to another MTA.

- *Mail retrieval agent (MRA)*: An MRA retrieves mails from a different system's mailbox, for instance, a remote server. After fetching the mail, it transfers that mail to the MDA.

POP3 Versus Web-Based E-Mail

POP3 E-Mail

POP3 (Post Office Protocol version 3) is the standard protocol for e-mail clients. This includes standalone clients, like Microsoft Outlook, and companion mail clients that are a part of other programs, like Microsoft Outlook Express and Mozilla Thunderbird. These clients use POP3 to download mail from a server to a local mailbox file.

General features of POP3 mail include:

- Uses a TCP connection to retrieve e-mail
- Supports message identifiers for disconnected systems
- Can be accessed from anywhere on the network using a variety of clients
- Open protocol defined by Internet standards like RFCs
- Does not require gateways for network connections

POP3 mail has the following advantages:

- Once mail is retrieved from the server, it resides on the local disk and can be read without an Internet connection.
- There is no size limit built into the protocol for sending or receiving messages, although many ISPs impose a limit.
- Attachments can be opened quickly once the message is downloaded to the local disk.

However, POP3 mail also has the following disadvantages:

- There is no virus protection in POP3 mail, so file attachments are often dangerous.
- Because messages are stored on the local disk, storage space can be an issue.
- If mail is deleted, it can be difficult to retrieve.
- Heavy use of POP3 mail may slow down network connections.

Web-Based E-Mail

Web-based e-mail allows users to send, receive, and manage e-mail through Web browsers. Popular providers include Gmail, Yahoo, and Hotmail. Using Web-based e-mail requires an active Internet connection at all times.

General features of Web-based e-mail include:

- Deleted items go into a trash folder, so they can be recovered within a few days.
- Antivirus software automatically scans all e-mail attachments.
- Filters can be used for incoming mail to sort it into appropriate folders.
- Many providers have advanced spam detection and blocking measures.
- POP3 can be used to retrieve e-mail from another service.

Web-based e-mail has the following advantages:

- Anywhere users have Web access, they can access their e-mail.
- Messages remain on the server, so they do not have to be downloaded to the local disk.
- Anonymous sign up increases user privacy.

However, it also has the following disadvantages:

- Unless additional software is installed, like Gmail Offline, an Internet connection is required to view messages.
- Advertisements appear, surrounding e-mails.
- Heavy use of Web-based e-mail may slow down network connections.
- Although most services provide a large amount of data for stored messages, there is no way to increase that size.

E-Mail Components

Aside from the message body, e-mail messages have several components.

Header

The header is the text at the beginning of the e-mail message, generated by the sender's e-mail client. As the message passes through mail programs on its way to the recipient, each program adds data to the header field. By viewing this field, the user can see the route the message took. Figure 2-1 shows a sample message header.

An e-mail header contains several fields, including:

- *Date*: A time stamp set by the sender of the message; because it is based on the time set on the sender's computer, it may not be accurate
- *To*: The address of the primary recipient
- *From*: The address of the sender
- *Subject*: A short description of the message
- *Cc (carbon copy)*: Additional recipients
- *Bcc (blind carbon copy)*: Additional recipients whose names do not appear to any other recipients

In addition, headers display the source IP address, filenames of any attachments, and a unique message number. All of this information can help determine the source of an e-mail, although it is not always reliable.

Figure 2-1 An e-mail message header contains several pieces of information regarding the e-mail message.

Header Field Names and Values

Every field begins with the field name followed by a colon. The field name can only be made up of standard alphanumeric characters. For example, take the following cc field:

```
cc: name@domain.com
```

Spaces and tabs are not allowed between the field name and the colon. The following example is not a valid field:

```
subject : text
```

The value of a field is all text next to the colon. In the following example, "name@domain.com, name2@domain2.com" is the value of the cc field:

```
cc: name@domain.com, name2@domain2.com
```

All data up until the next field name is considered the value of the field. Any number of spaces and line breaks can be included. The following field has the same value as the example above:

```
cc:

name@domain.com,

name2@domain2.com
```

A space after the colon is not required, although it is preferred. For instance, the following is valid:

```
subject:text
```

Received: Headers

The received: headers of an e-mail indicate the source of the e-mail and the route the message took from the sender to the recipient. The last listed received: header indicates the original sender of the e-mail. For example:

```
Received: from targetsite.com (loca4242. targetsite.com

[xxx.xxx.xxx.xxx]) by postbox.targetsite.com (6.11.3/6.11.3) with

ESMTP id B50x678GHJL
```

The header of a typical spam e-mail has less detail about the source of the message and provides no details about the sender. For example:

```
<user@server.com>; Thur, 7 Jan 2000 21:38:03 - 0600 (CST)
```

The top received: header shows the final server to handle the e-mail. A spam message's top received: header has extra data such as:

```
Received: from fantasycards.com ([xxx.xxx.xxx.xxx])

By postbox. targetsite.com (6.11.3/6.11.3) for <george@

targetsite.com>; Thu, 20 Nov 2000 21:38:04 -0600 (CST)
```

Other Headers

The from: header in spam e-mails is generally false and, therefore, is of no use.

The message-ID: header is an identification number, followed by @ and the sending server's name, for example:

```
Message-ID: <3A2EDAFA.F4735272@myisp.com>
```

A spam's message-ID: header usually does not include the sending server's name after the @:

```
Message-ID: <00000ee45f1f$00003dcf$00004947@>
```

Reading Headers

The following shows how to read the headers using different e-mail clients:

- Hotmail
  - Login to the Hotmail account.
  - Click the **Options** link on the top navigation bar.
  - Click the **Mail Display Settings** link.
  - Change the **Message Headers** option to **Full**.
  - Click the **OK** button.
- Yahoo! Mail
  - Log into the Yahoo Mail account.
  - Click the **Options** link on the navigation bar.
  - Click the **General Preferences** link.
  - Click **Messages** and select **Show All Headers**.
  - Click the **Save** button.
- Netscape
  - Open the **View** menu.
  - Click on **Page Source**.
  - Copy the contents of the window.
- Gmail
  - Log into the Gmail account.
  - Open an e-mail.
  - Click on the down arrow next to the date of the e-mail.
  - Click the **Show original** link.
  - A new window will open with the headers and body of the message.
- XtraMail
  - Log into the XtraMail account.
  - Click **Options** in the left navigation bar.
  - Click the **Display** button.
  - Change the **Message Headers** option to **Full**.
  - Click the **OK** button.
- Thunderbird
  - Open the **View** menu.
  - Click **Headers**.
  - Select **All**.
- Outlook Express 4, 5, 6
  - Open the message in its own window.
  - Open the **File** menu.
  - Click **Properties**.
  - Click the **Details** tab.
  - Click **Message Source**.
  - Highlight, copy, and paste everything from the window.

- Outlook 98 and 2000
  - Open the message in its own window.
  - Open the **View** menu.
  - Click **Options**.
  - Copy the text in the Internet headers window and then paste it into a separate document.
  - Close the **Options** window.
- Microsoft Exchange
  - Open the **File** menu.
  - Click **Properties**.
  - Click the **Details** tab.
  - Click **Message Source**.
  - Highlight, copy, and paste everything from the **Message Source**.

Address List

An address list is a sequence of any number of e-mail addresses, including zero. This list can include the following items:

- Address groups
- Phrases
- Bracketed addresses (addresses between < and > symbols)
- Routes (domain names following @ symbols indicating the route the message took)
- Encoded addresses (addresses in *name@server* format)
- Encoded domain names

Responses and Threading

The recipient of a message often sends another message in reply. This could go to just the sender of the original message, or to the sender and all other recipients. When this happens, the references field in the header contains the message identifiers of the other messages in the conversation. These identifiers are bracketed, meaning they are between < and > symbols.

The "in reply to" field contains the same information as these reference field message identifiers.

Attachments

One of the most useful features of e-mail is the ability to easily send files over the Internet. After a message has been received, an icon is shown for each attached file corresponding to the file type. Based on this file type, the local operating system will decide what program to use when opening the file. It is very important to be careful when opening executable files, because even if they come from a trusted sender, they could contain viruses.

Signatures

The sender has the option to attach a signature to outgoing e-mails. This signature is a few lines automatically appended to the end of the message body. It can contain any content the user wishes to include, such as the full name of the sender, physical contact address, or a legal disclaimer.

A signature is stored in a file on the sender's local disk. The filename is based on the e-mail program used. Signature files on Windows machines are commonly named signature.sig or signature.txt, while on UNIX systems, .sig and .signatures are commonly used.

Configuring and Testing an E-Mail Server

E-mail servers are programs that exchange e-mail messages with e-mail clients and other servers. They are composed of the following parts:

- A storage area that stores the mail of local users
- Rules determining what mail should be accepted and what mail should be rejected
- A list of users
- Communication modules monitoring the exchange of mail

UNIX E-Mail Server

There are several UNIX-specific e-mail servers, including mail, mailx, qmail, Pine, and Sendmail. All of these keep log files and configuration files that can be used in the event of an investigation. Sendmail, in particular, creates its configuration data in /etc/sendmail.cf. The syslogd file describes the events that Sendmail should record.

Microsoft Exchange 2000 E-Mail Server

Microsoft Exchange 2000 e-mail server uses the Microsoft Extensible Storage Engine (ESE) to provide e-mail services. Exchange records data in a transaction record. A checkpoint file or marker is inserted in the transaction record to mark the most recent point at which the database was written to the disk. These files allow the e-mail administrator to retrieve deleted or lost e-mail messages.

Novell GroupWise E-Mail Server

The Novell GroupWise e-mail server software has approximately 25 databases for e-mails. Every database is stored in the OFUSER directory object, with a filename based on the username followed by a unique identifier and a .db file extension. GroupWise mailboxes make it easy to retrieve specific data.

E-Mail Encryption and Authentication

Encryption is the only way to truly secure e-mail messages against sniffing and spoofing. However, this makes it impossible for e-mail servers to examine attachments for viruses, because the servers cannot read these encrypted files.

All e-mail encryption approaches use public-key encryption to protect messages. The e-mail encryption package generates a private key for the user and a public key that can be given to the sender. If the message can be decoded, it proves that it came from a source with the public key.

Both parties must use the same system in order to exchange encrypted e-mail. The two most popular systems are Secure Multipurpose Internet Mail Extensions (S/MIME) and Pretty Good Privacy (PGP). PGP is not as available for all users and not as user friendly. S/MIME is a standard used by numerous vendors that requires external certificates. Both systems are available for free, although S/MIME requires the user to possess an X.509 digital certificate setup. This allows the root certificate authorities to create a digital certificate that has transitive dependencies between various organizations. End users can have difficulty acquiring fixed digital certificates due to the time and financial costs required to administer them.

CenturionMail

CenturionMail is a Windows-based utility that integrates with Microsoft Outlook to allow users to transfer encrypted information through e-mail. This encrypted information is sent along with an attachment. Once the receiver runs the attachment, it will prompt for a password that will decrypt the message.

Encrypted files can be sent using any user-defined file extension. CenturionMail uses 256-bit AES for strong encryption. It maintains a password manager that securely stores and manages all passwords used by different recipients, and provides password hints to the recipients should they forget their password. It also contains a shredder program to completely delete unencrypted files.

Kerberos

Kerberos is a widely used Internet authentication protocol. A Kerberos Authentication Server (KAS) issues and verifies client credentials. It is platform independent and used mostly by UNIX systems and the Microsoft Active Directory service. Kerberos authentication follows these steps:

1. When a client logs onto a system, the client sends a request to the KAS for credentials.
2. Once the client is verified, the KAS allows the user to establish a connection. It returns a session key that will be used to encrypt further service requests in the current session.
3. The user or client must provide that key to KAS for any network connection.
4. KAS provides a session ticket that will be valid for that particular session.
5. Finally, the client issues a service key to the service provider to establish a connection to access the network resource.

Hushmail

Hushmail is a Web-based mail program that provides encryption. Its services include:

- PGP-encrypted e-mail
- File storage
- Efficient domain service
- Hush Messenger instant messaging

Hushmail has the following key advantages:

- Hides IP addresses in e-mail headers
- Highly secure
- Free

However, it has the following disadvantages:

- Very small inbox for free accounts
- Paid membership required to use protocols like IMAP and POP3

Pretty Good Privacy (PGP)

PGP is a free and powerful encryption program for both files and e-mails. It runs on multiple platforms and provides features like message encryption, digital signatures to verify a sender's identity, and data compression. The RSA algorithm is used for message encryption, key transport, and digital signatures; IDEA is used for bulk message encryptions; and MD5 is used for computing the message digests.

A PGP signature is different for every message, because it is based on both the message and the user's secret key. Each key is a very long number, such as the following example PGP signature:

```
mQCNAzGvwGAAAAEEAMQXIO6gfdoZzy2Ngdqua6Zf6q4Bfdotc8qGHk9RncuEHSBf
2DrqYrkVmn6cANJp/HdBkJH39LcKybOGbxiahmjVnngPp+PzvX8+Wi7kQ5NP267S
OJIituePxuklEQ5pqywHw8yxtOGIqLjkJtb/pRvZyiC0Cyw1bjnbPFHw2SetAAUR
tCZSb2JpbiBXaGl0dGxlIDxmaXJzdHByQG96ZW1haWwuY29tLmF1PokAlQMFEDGv
WGE52zxR8NknrQEBbV0D/1gJSldscj2bFJ0uD9LOY+LSTj71yxdONZ3cycPZ+3zp
ShCNcsqNAGvHXDtqcGQrNrxHmYqnKBaJ/+46n/FSkDnt/bvEAb105m+6T5oTK8h+
MaaVuvdcphwKfIPQbIoI6LcmtwSd0cyBBndp+O+02x0xhcd2Qx7Gni7J+fz8mm0y
=Ysjn
```

Secure Hive

Secure Hive is a file encryption tool that uses digital signatures to secure archive files and documents. It is able to integrate with Microsoft Office applications and supports a command-line interface for batch processing files and archives. Secure Hive's graphical interface is shown in Figure 2-2.

Source: http://www.securehive.com/images/encrypt.jpg. Accessed 2004.

Figure 2-2   Secure Hive is a simple file encryption tool.

Softalk WorkgroupMail

WorkgroupMail is a mail server that provides spam filtering, content filtering, server-based virus protection, and shared address book functions.

After downloading the program, a user should follow these steps to install it:

1. Open setup.exe, which will open the **Welcome** screen shown in Figure 2-3. Click the **Next** button.

Figure 2-3   Click the **Next** button on the **Welcome** screen.

2. Read the license agreement, shown in Figure 2-4, and click the **Accept** button to continue.

Figure 2-4   Accept the license agreement.

3. On the next screen, click the **Install WorkgroupMail as an executable program** button, as shown in Figure 2-5, and click the **Next** button.

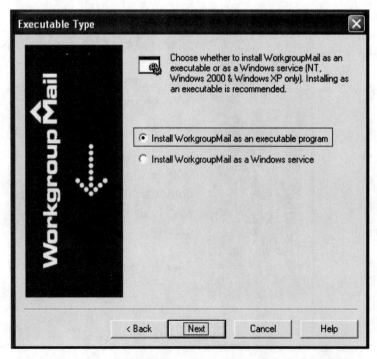

Figure 2-5   Install WorkgroupMail as an executable program.

4. Select a destination folder to install files, as shown in Figure 2-6, and then click the **Next** button.

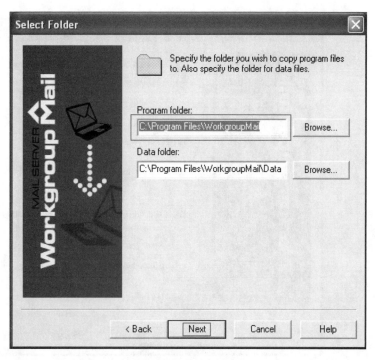

Figure 2-6   Select a destination folder.

5. Click the **Standalone mail server** button, as shown in Figure 2-7, and then click the **Next** button.

Figure 2-7   Configure WorkgroupMail as a standalone mail server.

6. Enter user details, as shown in Figure 2-8, and then click the **Next** button.

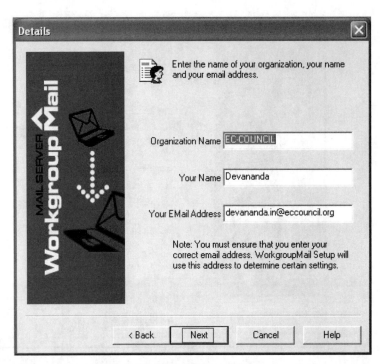

Figure 2-8   Enter user details.

7. Enter the IP addresses to use as the primary and secondary DNS servers, as shown in Figure 2-9, and then click the **Next** button.

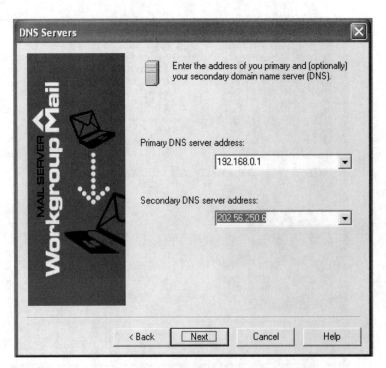

Figure 2-9   Enter the primary and secondary DNS server IP addresses.

8. Read the summary page shown in Figure 2-10, and then click the **Finish** button.

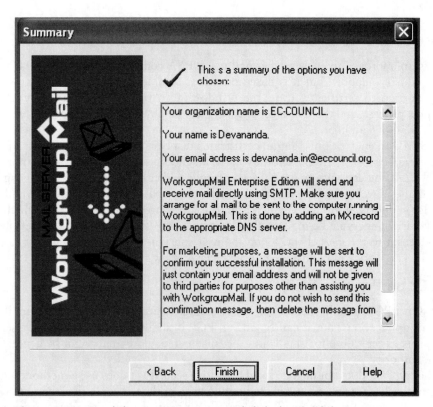

Figure 2-10 Read the summary page and click the **Finish** button.

Configuring Outlook Express

Microsoft Outlook Express is included with most Windows installations. To configure it, a user should open it and then follow these steps:

1. In the **Internet Accounts** box, click **New Outlook Express account**, and then click **Properties**.
2. To identify the new mail account by a name other than the default name, type the desired name in the **Mail Account** box. This name is known as the friendly name for the account.
3. Click the **Connection** tab.
   - If a local area network (LAN) is used: check the **Always connect to this account** checkbox, click **Local Area Network**, and then click the **OK** button.
   - To add a different type of connection, such as a modem or an ISDN line: check the **Always connect to this account** checkbox, click the **Add** button, and then follow the prompts to configure the required connection type.
4. Click the **Finish** button.

E-Mail Protocols

A protocol is a set of rules that govern the exchange of information over networks. The mail client and mail server can exchange data with each other using various protocols, including the following:

- S/MIME
- PGP

- SMTP
- IMAP
- POP3

Multipurpose Internet Mail Extensions (MIME)/Secure MIME

S/MIME is an approach to encrypted e-mail using RSA commercial public keys. It is a free standard that has extensive industry support, but it is based on fixed, commercial X.509 certificates. Companies can generate their own nonrooted certificates using the Windows Certificate Server service or Open SSL. However, it is a very complex process, and these new certificates must be physically exchanged between organizations that wish to securely mail one another.

To use S/MIME encryption, a digital certificate must be acquired from a certificate authority and installed in the user's e-mail client. S/MIME is not, by itself, an encryption algorithm or a standard. Some S/MIME executions use RC2 40-bit encryption, which is very fragile and can be broken quickly using brute-force methods, but it was the highest level of security that the United States would allow to be sold abroad at the time of its development. It also supports 56-bit DES, which is marginally better, and Triple-DES, which offers 168-bit security.

To make use of encrypted e-mail on the client side, the user downloads a certificate from a reliable provider and introduces it to the mail client. Later, the user encrypts e-mail messages sent to others, which include the user's public key. This will be installed in the receiver's key ring.

Pretty Good Privacy (PGP)

PGP and OpenPGP e-mail encryption use a standard protocol to encrypt e-mail. PGP is not built in to most e-mail applications, but it can be added. PGP is slightly less intuitive and user friendly than S/MIME. However, it is easier to use for small sites, because personal key pairs can be generated without the need of a certificate authority.

Even though PGP does not include fixed transitive security, it does use a methodology called "a web of trust." Those who use the system sign the posted public keys of those people that they know face-to-face, in order to confirm the identity of the person. This mutually authenticates users and requires substantial participation to work. It works out extremely well for business associates, because they can mutually certify each other.

Simple Mail Transfer Protocol (SMTP)

Simple Mail Transfer Protocol (SMTP) allows mail to be sent from the source to the destination without any data loss. Communications are transferred using interprocess communication environments (IPCEs), allowing one process to communicate with the other directly. All IPCEs are connected to one another.

In SMTP, the communication starts with a mail request. The sending server establishes a two-way transmission channel with the receiver. SMTP commands allow these two servers to communicate. The receiver acknowledges the requests with an OK reply. The sending server also transfers an RCPT command to designate the mail recipient. If the receiver does not give an OK reply, then the mail is rejected.

SMTP has the following vulnerabilities:

- Remote attackers can send malicious server response messages to SMTP components of servers and Exchange routing engines, which can execute arbitrary code.
- Attackers can use DNS response messages to affect the server applications. If this attack is successful, the attacker gains control over the server.

To counteract these vulnerabilities, administrators should use a firewall to block TCP network traffic. TCP network traffic should be blocked for Windows Server 2000 SMTP components, which handle DNS lookups.

Internet Message Access Protocol (IMAP)

Internet Message Access Protocol (IMAP) is a protocol used to access e-mail or bulletin board messages that are stored on a shared mail server. It allows the client e-mail application to access remote message backups as if they were local. An e-mail saved on an IMAP server can be accessed anywhere, with no need to relocate messages.

Post Office Protocol Version 3 (POP3)

POP3 (Post Office Protocol version 3) supports offline message access, in which the messages are downloaded and are then removed from the mail server.

POP3 uses case-insensitive keyword commands, ending with a pair of CRLFs (carriage return/line feeds). Keywords are three to four characters in length, and can be followed by a single space and then any arguments. Responses in the POP3 are comprised of a status indicator and a keyword. All responses also terminate with a pair of CRLFs. Responses can be a maximum of 512 characters, including the terminating CRLF. There are two status indicators: positive (+OK) and negative (−ERR). These indicators must always be presented in capital letters.

When the TCP connection is established, the POP3 server sends a response to the connection request, and the session enters the authorization state. In this state, the client has to show its identity to the POP3 server. The server then obtains the resources related to the client's mail drop, and the session enters the transaction state. Here, the client requests actions from the POP3 server. When the client sends the **quit** command, the session enters the update state. The POP3 server releases the resources obtained during the transaction state and quits, closing the TCP connection.

Client-Server Architecture

The LAN and Internet exchange data from a central server to a set of connected client computers. This configuration is called the client-server architecture. The server runs an e-mail server programs such as Exchange Server 2000, GroupWise, or Sendmail to offer e-mail services. Client computers use e-mail programs such as Outlook or Thunderbird to connect to the e-mail server in order to send and receive e-mail messages.

Client-Server Architecture in a LAN

In a LAN, the e-mail server is usually a component of the local network. LAN e-mail programs are company specific and provide limited features. For example, a LAN e-mail system does not permit users to create addresses of their choice.

Client-Server Architecture in the Internet

An organization that provides e-mail services, such as Gmail or Hotmail, runs its e-mail server on the Internet. Any user can use these services by connecting to the Internet and providing a username and a password.

E-Mail Security Risks

Spam

Spam is any commercially driven, unwanted bulk mailing. Spammers have developed a range of spamming techniques, including e-mail spam, instant messaging spam, Usenet newsgroup spam, Web search engine spam, Web log spam, and mobile messaging spam.

E-mail spam involves transmitting identical, or nearly identical, unwanted messages to a huge number of recipients. Most e-mail programs and servers have filters to detect spam, but modern spammers have created tricks to bypass these filters.

Spammers acquire e-mail addresses through a variety of means, including Usenet postings, DNS listings, Web pages, and guessing names at familiar domains. One technique, known as e-pending, involves guessing e-mail addresses using specific names, such as residents in a community. Many spammers employ programs called Web spiders to harvest e-mail addresses from Web pages. However, it is possible to deceive these programs by replacing the @ symbol with another symbol, such as # or even the word *at*, when posting an e-mail address.

E-mail spammers are careful to hide the origin of their messages. They can achieve this by spoofing e-mail addresses, which is similar to Internet Protocol spoofing. Spammers alter e-mail messages to make it appear as if they are originating from another address.

Open-relay servers use old, less secure versions of SMTP, so spammers use them frequently. As open relays are becoming obsolete, spammers are using broadband connectivity to hack home computers, infecting them with viruses and using them to send spam, much like a DDoS attack. Hackers sell access control codes to spammers so that they can easily exploit systems.

SMTP protocol has no built-in authentication mechanism that can stop spam on the Internet, and it does not reliably identify the sender. It is difficult to trace spammers, and the total bandwidth loss cannot be calculated.

Protection Against Spam

The following methods can be effective in reducing spam:

- *SMTP server authentication:* This method sets the SMTP server to discard mail from unauthorized users. It will not allow messages from open relays. Closed relays can send e-mail only to users who are already authenticated or already allowed based on their IP address.

- *Host-based and network-based authentication:* In this method, the e-mail server relays e-mail to recipients who are in the hosted domain list or inside the local IP domain. This can be a problem for users who travel frequently.

- *Web e-mail interfaces:* This method provides a secure Web interface for private e-mail servers. Web e-mail interfaces provide a secure mechanism for traveling users.

- *POP before SMTP authentication:* In this method, users who have made a valid POP connection are then allowed to make an SMTP connection. Therefore, as long as a user can retrieve his or her mail from a server, he or she should be allowed to send e-mail using that same server.

- *Systematic spam prevention:* This method stops spammers from sending mail and blocks mail from exploited relays. Some of these methods may examine e-mail messages for indications that they are spam and block them if they are.

- *Mail abuse prevention system (MAPS):* This system scans e-mail Web interfaces, which are open relays, and sends a copy of spammed messages to itself through a Web server. It thus creates a blacklist of specific spammed e-mails, allowing the user to block spam by checking the mail list of spam copies in the database. It is very effective, but also very expensive.

Spam Filters

A spam filter identifies and then blocks or diverts incoming spam. This software can be installed on a mail server or the user's machine. In addition to scanning the messages themselves, spam filters check e-mail senders against lists of known spammers. Messages can be filtered based on the following criteria:

- Sender's e-mail address
- Particular words in the subject or message body
- Types of attachments
- Signature words

Spam can be filtered using either the peer-to-peer method or the AI technique. In the peer-to-peer method, users report and delete spam messages using a **Spam** button in their e-mail clients. This is reported back to a central server. Once a sufficient number of users report that message as spam, it is deleted from everyone else's inbox.

With the AI technique, sophisticated spam filters search for keywords and try to decipher the overall meaning of the message. This can be very effective in reducing false positives.

Hoaxes

An e-mail hoax is simply a lie propagated through forwarded e-mails. It is fairly common for innocent users to pass these false messages along, thinking they are helping others avoid some sort of threat, such as a computer virus. In some cases, these hoax e-mails contain viruses themselves.

When receiving an e-mail warning of some threat, especially if it has instructions to pass it along to as many people as possible, users should check the e-mail's facts. The easiest way is to simply perform a Web search on its claims and see if it has been widely reported as a hoax. Figure 2-11 shows an example of a hoax e-mail.

Phishing

Phishing (possibly derived from "password harvesting fishing") is an e-mail security threat where an attacker tries to obtain sensitive information such as passwords and credit card details using false e-mails. The attacker can then use this information to steal a user's identity. Users must be trained to resist phishing attacks.

Phishing usually involves re-creating a legitimate Web site to trick users into entering sensitive data, thinking that they are on the actual, trusted site. For instance, a common phishing e-mail pretends to be from a major

```
Subject: [Fwd: Beware of the Budweiser virus--really!]

This information came from Microsoft yesterday morning. Please pass it on to anyone you know who has
access to the Internet. You may receive an apparently harmless Budweiser Screensaver, If you do, DO NOT
OPEN IT UNDER ANY CIRCUMSTANCES, but delete it immediately. Once opened, you will lose EVERYTHING on your
PC. Your hard disk will be completely destroyed and the person who sent you the message will have access
to your name and password via the Internet.

As far as we know, the virus was circulated yesterday morning. It's a new virus, and extremely dangerous.
Please copy this information and e-mail it to everyone in your address book. We need to do all we can to
block his virus. AOL has confirmed how dangerous it is, and there is no Antivirus program as yet which is
capable of destroying it.

Please take all the necessary precautions, and pass this information on to your friends, acquaintances
and work colleagues.

End of message.

EMAILCHIEF
```

Figure 2-11   This is a hoax e-mail. Note that it gives specific instructions to "pass this information on to your friends, acquaintances and work colleagues."

bank's customer support division, asking users to click a link and enter their usernames and passwords. The link leads to a site that looks like the bank's real site, but the login information is forwarded to the attacker.

Snarfing

Snarfing is when an attacker intercepts e-mails and extracts confidential information from them.

Malware

Malware is any computer code that causes undesired outcomes. These outcomes include:

- Establishing a communication link with a remote system and permitting unauthorized access
- Crashing the PC or program
- Redirecting the browser to unwanted Web sites
- Helping an attacker take over the system

To avoid malware, users should be certain to run all e-mail attachments through virus scanners before opening them.

Viruses

A virus is a type of program that can duplicate itself by making copies. It is triggered by a user running a program, and it quickly replicates itself. A user might transmit it over a network or execute it on removable media. Viruses can also spread to other computers by corrupting publicly accessible or shared files.

The most common targets of viruses are executable files that have application software or are parts of the operating system. They can also corrupt the executable boot sectors of floppy disks, script files of application programs, and documents with macro scripts.

Gateway Virus Scanners An e-mail gateway virus scanner can be a more practical solution than installing virus scanners on every computer unit. The gateway virus scanner catches viruses as they enter through the gateway. These need to be updated frequently in order to always catch newer viruses. The majority of gateway virus scanners also include spam filters.

There are several different gateway virus scanners, differing in the pace at which the vendors discover new viruses and deploy new virus definitions, how easy they are to use, and the cost of the software. They all use roughly the same methods for detecting viruses.

Outlook Viruses Outlook and Outlook Express have unique security troubles because of their tight integration with Windows. These viruses can implement scripts in e-mail messages that can cause significant damage.

Most Outlook viruses go through the user's Outlook contacts and then e-mail themselves to all the addresses present in the address book. These malicious messages appear as if the infected user has sent them, so the user's associates are likely to trust the messages and may even open attachments. If the user has S/MIME public keys, the virus can even encrypt itself and send itself to receivers who accept only encrypted mail.

Worms

A computer worm is a self-replicating computer program. Unlike a virus, it requires no human intervention to replicate. They are often designed to exploit the file transmission capabilities found on many computers. Like a virus, a worm may be designed to perform malicious activities, such as delete files on a host system, send documents via e-mail, or transmit other executables. If nothing else, a worm can cause loss just with the network traffic created by its duplication.

Trojan

Trojan horse attacks can breach computer security and cause serious threats. A victim may not only be under attack but may also be used as an intermediary to attack others.

Trojans are attached to innocent-looking files. For example, if the user downloads a movie or a music file, opening it could release a program that erases the hard drive or compromises sensitive data. A Trojan could install a backdoor, making the user's computer a server that the attacker can access and control.

E-Mail Spoofing

E-mail spoofing involves altering an e-mail to make it appear to come from a different source. SMTP does not have a built-in authentication mechanism, which makes e-mail spoofing common.

An e-mail server can be programmed to refuse SMTP connections from any e-mail server that doesn't have a legitimate registered domain name. In some cases, it is even possible to reject mail from all but a few trusted domains of business partners. These methods will not only decrease spoofed mail but will greatly decrease the spread of viruses and worms from unknown sources. E-mail encoding can also be used to protect the contents of e-mail and confirm that the message originated from the user who transmitted the public key.

Attachment Security

While attachments are a very convenient way to transfer files, they also pose a danger for the propagation of malware. Multipurpose Internet Mail Extension (MIME) is an IETF protocol for encrypting and sending files along with attributes that identify how the files should be decrypted. MIME can also be used to send multimedia content over Web pages.

Scan and Block All E-Mail Attachments

It is easy to block e-mails with e-mail servers, but it does not protect against spoofing. E-mail servers with open access, such as Exchange, have the ability to block attachments. When using an e-mail server that does not contain a blocking function, a UNIX-based relay server can be installed between the e-mail server and the Internet. MX (Mail Exchange) servers should be installed to send mail to the relay server. User machines should be configured to permit the MX records to transfer e-mails from the user's system to the relay server and from the relay server to the administrative e-mail server.

Server settings can be changed to be more lenient or strict in allowing attachments. Attachments can also be decoded and moved to the FTP directory of the mail server so that the administrator can inspect them.

Permit Precise Attachments

End users should be aware of the attachments they send and receive. Mail servers can be configured to permit only certain, specified attachments. The user may only expect certain file types, like Office documents or .pdf files, and the server can block the rest. Office documents can still contain malicious macros, but most illegitimate attachments will be eliminated.

Use Third-Party E-Mail Servers

By transforming an e-mail server into an e-mail firewall, most e-mail security problems can be eliminated. E-mail firewalls scan e-mails for harmful scripts, block e-mail attachments from open relays, and block mail from illegitimate DNS servers.

Forcing POP3 traffic to pass through the firewall increases security. Corporate users should not be allowed to use personal e-mail accounts, which would allow unchecked attachments to enter the corporate network.

Block Attachments

Operating systems have built-in mechanisms to identify and block certain attachments. The following file types can be dangerous and should be blocked:

- Executable (.exe)
- Command (.com)
- Command (.cmd)
- Program information file (.pif)
- Screensaver (.scr)
- JavaScript (.js or .jse)
- VBScript (.vb, .vbe, .vbs)
- HTML application (.hta)
- Microsoft Installer package (.msi, .mst, .msp)
- Registry files (.reg)
- Program links (.lnk)

Microsoft Outlook has a feature to quarantine executable mail attachments. Attachments with the following file extensions should be blocked without regard to the sender:

- Extension for MS Access projects (.ade)
- MS Access project (.adp)
- Class module for Microsoft Visual Basic (.bas)
- Compiled HTML help file (.chm)
- Control Panel extension (.cpl)
- Security certificate (.crt)
- Help file (.hlp)
- Setup information (.inf)
- Internet Naming Service (.ins)
- Internet communication settings (.isp)
- Microsoft Access add-in program (.mda)
- Microsoft Access database (.mdb)
- Microsoft Access MDE database (.mde)
- Microsoft Access wizard program (.mdz)
- Microsoft Common Console document (.msc)
- Visual Test source files (.mst)
- Microsoft Visual Test compiled script (also used by PhotoCD) (.pcd)
- Windows script component (.sct)
- Shell scrap object (.shs)
- Internet shortcut (.url)
- Windows script component (.wsc)
- Windows Script file (.wsf)
- Windows Script Host settings file (.wsh)

Network administrators working on cross-platform applications often use the Perl language for administrative scripting. Its .pl and .pls extensions are as dangerous as the .js and .vbs scripting extensions. If a hacker determines that the administrator is using Perl, the system can be attacked. This is why it is necessary to only allow attachments that are known to the user and to strictly block other file extensions.

E-Mail Bombing

E-mail bombing involves transferring a huge amount of e-mail to the victim, crashing the victim's e-mail account. This can also cause the service provider to delete the account, due to too much incoming traffic clogging the network.

One way to do this is to subscribe the victim to a large number of mailing lists. Some of these lists produce only a few messages per day, while others produce a great deal. Another, more direct way is to create a message, entering the e-mail address of the victim numerous times in the To: field, and press the **Send** button many times. For instance, entering the e-mail address 20 times and pressing the **Send** button 40 times sends 800 e-mail messages to the victim's inbox. There are numerous hacking tools that automate the process of e-mail bombing. These tools send numerous e-mails from many diverse e-mail servers, which make it very difficult for the victim to take countermeasures or even identify the attacker.

Increasing E-Mail Security

An administrator can follow these basic guidelines to increase e-mail security:

- Text-based mails are safer than HTML e-mails.
- The preview feature of the e-mail client must be disabled. Users should be required to manually open e-mails.
- E-mail received from unidentified sources must be deleted.
- E-mails requesting sensitive information must be verified for authenticity by checking with the company's Web site. Employees should open e-mails received from the organization's technical support team only after they have confirmed their authenticity with other employees.
- Each attachment must be checked for the presence of a virus or worm. E-mail attachments must never be directly opened from an e-mail application; they must be saved to disk and then scanned for viruses. If the sender's address, name, and other information do not seem familiar or cannot be verified, it is better to ignore the attachment. Take extra care with files with executable extensions (discussed previously in this chapter).
- It is recommended not to use e-mail addresses as usernames on external Web sites.
- Use a personal e-mail address for personal activities, such as online shopping.
- When giving out an e-mail address, do so in the form of plaintext rather than hyperlinks.
- Spam filters must be implemented.
- Personal use of e-mail must be governed by the organization's acceptable use policy.

Quarantining Suspicious E-Mail

A quarantine system diverts suspicious mail, like spam, to a predefined folder. The messages in quarantine will be available for a set amount of time, usually four weeks, after which they will be deleted. The user can also manually delete them. This can significantly reduce the space taken up by e-mail accounts, as well as reduce e-mail security risks.

Vulnerability Checks

Vulnerability checks assess the performance of an e-mail system. These checks carry out the following tests:

- Testing if the system will accept e-mail with long subjects
- Testing if the system will accept attachments containing executable files with no filenames
- Testing if the system can block e-mails with attachments having long filenames
- Testing the functionality of antivirus software

Tools for E-Mail Security

ClipSecure

ClipSecure, shown in Figure 2-12, is a freeware encryption tool that provides security to e-mail clients and other text-based applications. This tool uses algorithms like AES, DES, Blowfish, Mars, and RC6 to encrypt text on the Windows clipboard, which can then be pasted in an e-mail message.

Crypto Anywhere

Crypto Anywhere is a portable, freeware e-mail program small enough to fit on a USB flash drive or even a floppy disk. This tool allows users to transfer mail from anywhere without any installation. It offers public-key encryption, in which a receiver needs decryption software, and self-decrypting messages, where the receiver just needs a password. Crypto Anywhere is shown in Figure 2-13 and uses encryption algorithms like RSA public-key encryption, the Twofish block cipher, and the ISAAC random number generator to provide a high level of security to e-mail messages.

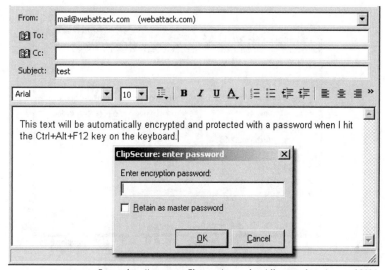

Source: http://www.snapfiles.com/screenshots/clipsecure.htm. Accessed 2004.

Figure 2-12   ClipSecure encrypts text using the Windows clipboard.

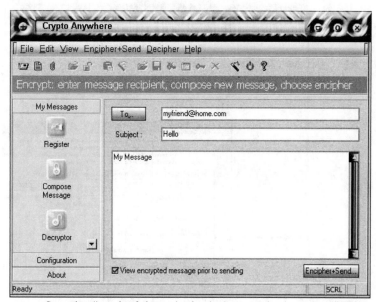

Source: http://www.bytefusion.com/products/ens/cryptoanywhere/encryptingmail123.htm.
Accessed 2004.

Figure 2-13   Crypto Anywhere is a small e-mail client that encrypts mail with no installation.

BCArchive

BCArchive allows users to compress groups of files and folders to a single encrypted file. It uses software like ZIP, RAR, and ARJ to compress files simply and securely, and then uses various encryption algorithms to protect the archive. To decompress the files, the user has to give the archive password. This tool uses strong encryption algorithms like Blowfish, IDEA, Triple-DES, and CAST5, as well as hash algorithms like SHA-1, MD5, RIPEMD-160, and asymmetric key algorithms.

BCArchive is shown in Figure 2-14 and has the following features:

- Creates an encrypted archive file that is protected by a password or another user's public key
- Creates self-extracting executables that do not require the recipient to have the BCArchive program

Cryptainer LE

Cryptainer LE is a free, 128-bit encryption tool that creates multiple 25-MB containers for encryption on the hard disk. A single password allows the user to modify, view, and hide all types of files. It is also portable, so it can be used on a removable drive without any installation. Cryptainer LE is shown in Figure 2-15.

Figure 2-14 BCArchive compresses and encrypts files and folders.

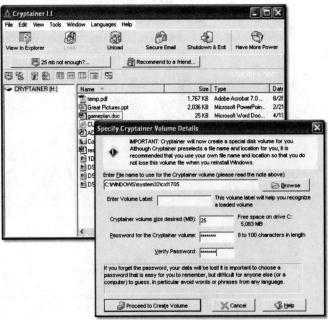

Source: http://www.snapfiles.com/screenshots/cryptainer.htm. Accessed 2004.

Figure 2-15 Cryptainer LE is a portable encryption tool.

GFI MailEssentials

GFI MailEssentials is a server-based e-mail security tool. Its Bayesian filter uses a mathematical formula to catch spam, using rules automatically downloaded from the vendor as well as by learning from messages marked as spam by its users. It allows the user to decide what to do with spam: delete it, forward it, or put it in a folder.

It also includes a list server for automating mass mailings, such as newsletters, as well as allowing users to subscribe and unsubscribe whenever they wish.

GFI MailEssentials integrates with Exchange and can use Microsoft Access or Microsoft SQL Server as the back end. It can record all incoming and outgoing mail to a Microsoft SQL Server database. A user can search archived mail for an exact message or a whole e-mail thread using the built-in Web interface.

Figure 2-16 shows GFI MailEssentials' configuration screen.

SpamAware

SpamAware is an add-on for Microsoft Outlook and Outlook Express. It uses Spam Assassin to keep a count of the mail entering the mailbox of a user, and it handles spam messages by either putting a mark in their subject lines or by forwarding them to trash folders. It also supports black and white lists, indicating which contacts are always safe and which are known spammers. SpamAware is shown in Figure 2-17.

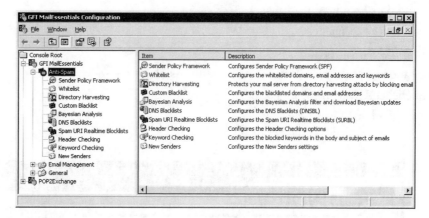

Figure 2-16   GFI MailEssentials provides spam filtering as well as list server functionality.

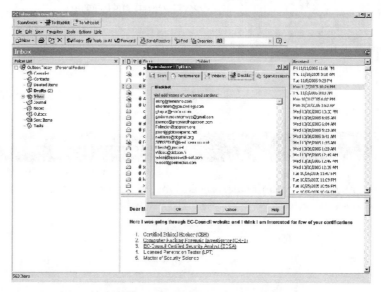

Figure 2-17   SpamAware either marks spam messages or puts them directly into trash folders.

Tracking an E-Mail

E-mail tracking helps users protect e-mail servers. The main uses of e-mail tracking are:

- Users can quarantine messages before they enter the network.
- Both incoming and outgoing mail can be filtered for inappropriate and unauthorized content.
- It can block viruses, spam, and suspicious mail.
- Lowering junk mail conserves system bandwidth and network resources.
- Administration and report generation can be simplified.
- E-mail tracking controls and facilitates policy enforcement.
- Tracking an e-mail ensures delivery of a message.
- Confidential data are protected.

ReadNotify

ReadNotify is a powerful tool that performs e-mail tracking services. It tells users when a sent e-mail is read, reopened, or forwarded. ReadNotify is shown in Figure 2-18 and provides a report containing the following:

- Time and date an e-mail was opened
- Location of the recipient
- IP address of the recipient
- E-mail address of the forwarded recipients (if possible)
- List of clicked URLs in the message
- Duration the e-mail was open

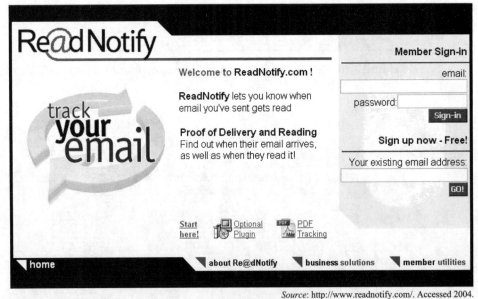

Source: http://www.readnotify.com/. Accessed 2004.

Figure 2-18   ReadNotify alerts users when their sent e-mails are read, reopened, or forwarded.

Chapter Summary

- E-mail, short for *electronic mail*, is the most common form of person-to-person communication over the Internet.

- POP3 (Post Office Protocol version 3) is the standard protocol for e-mail clients.

- Web-based e-mail allows users to send, receive, and manage e-mail through Web browsers.

- The e-mail header is the text at the beginning of the e-mail message, generated by the sender's e-mail client.

- It is very important to be careful when opening executable files that have been sent as an attachment, because even if they come from a trusted sender, they could contain viruses.

- E-mail servers are programs that exchange e-mail messages with e-mail clients and other servers.

- Encryption is the only way to truly secure e-mail messages against sniffing and spoofing.

- S/MIME is an approach to encrypted e-mail using RSA commercial public keys.

- PGP and OpenPGP e-mail encryption use a standard protocol to encrypt e-mail.

- Simple Mail Transfer Protocol (SMTP) allows mail to be sent from the source to the destination without any data loss.

- Internet Message Access Protocol (IMAP) is a protocol used to access e-mail or bulletin board messages that are stored on a shared mail server.

- Spam is any commercially driven, unwanted bulk mailing.

- Phishing is an e-mail security threat where an attacker tries to obtain sensitive information such as passwords and credit card details using false e-mails.

- E-mail spoofing involves altering an e-mail to make it appear to come from a different source.

Review Questions

1. What are the elements of an e-mail?

_____

_____

_____

_____

2. What are the different types of e-mail?

_____

_____

_____

_____

3. What is the difference between Web-based e-mail and POP3 e-mail?

_____

_____

_____

_____

4. What are the components of an e-mail header?

_____

_____

_____

_____

5. What attachments should be blocked, or at least handled with care?

_____

_____

_____

_____

6. What are the elements of e-mail encryption?

_____

_____

_____

_____

7. What are common e-mail protocols?

_____

_____

_____

_____

8. What is e-mail spoofing?

_____

_____

_____

9. What is spam?

_____

_____

_____

_____

10. What is e-mail bombing?

_____

_____

_____

_____

11. What are some tools that can be used to secure e-mail?

_____

_____

_____

_____

Hands-On Projects

1. Use Spam Reader to extend Outlook functionality with a Bayesian spam filter.

   - Navigate to Chapter 2 of the Student Resource Center.
   - Install and launch the Spam Reader program.
   - Click **Good Email** to select useful mail.
   - Click **Junk Email** to select the junk/spam e-mail.
   - Click **Black List** and then click **Add**.
   - Type the name and e-mail address of a known spammer and click **OK**.
   - Click **OK** in the main window to finish setup.

2. Use Spytech Spam Agent to remove spam and indicate when there is new mail waiting by playing a sound or pop-up message.

   - Navigate to Chapter 2 of the Student Resource Center.
   - Install and launch the Spytech Spam Agent program.
   - Click **General Options**.
   - Click the **Startup Options** tab, select the necessary startup options, and click **OK**.
   - Click the **Account Information** tab, fill in all information about the e-mail account to be used, and click **OK**.
   - Click the **Thread Priority** tab, select an option to set its priority, and click **OK**.

3. Use SpamExperts Desktop to filter the e-mail in a POP3/IMAP account for both spam and viruses.

   - Navigate to Chapter 2 of the Student Resource Center.
   - Install and launch the SpamExperts Desktop program.
   - Click **Edit** and then **Settings**.
   - Click the **General Settings** tab and view the details.
   - Click the **Intercepted Email Applications** tab and view the details.
   - Click the **Periodic Retrieval** tab and view the details.
   - Click **Blocked Senders**, right-click on the window, and select **Add New Address** to add addresses to be blocked.
   - Click **Allowed Senders**, right-click on the window, and select **Add New Address** to add trusted addresses.

4. Use ReadNotify to send an e-mail and track the usage, location, time, and date the e-mail is opened.

   - Visit *http://www.readnotify.com*.
   - Sign up for a free account.
   - Open your primary e-mail program.
   - Create a new message.

- In the **To:** field, enter your secondary e-mail address, followed by ".readnotify.com." For example, if your secondary e-mail address is *user@domain.com*, send the mail message to *user@domain.com.readnotify.com*.

- Log on to the secondary account and read the message.

- Forward this e-mail to any other e-mail accounts you have.

- Visit *http://www.readnotify.com*.

- Log on.

- View the tracking information of the e-mail that you sent.

Authentication, Encryption, and Digital Signatures

Objectives

After completing this chapter, you should be able to:

- Understand authentication using encryption and digital signatures
- Understand message authentication using cryptography
- Analyze popular encryption schemes
- Understand the IPSec architecture
- Understand the certificate encryption process in digital certificates
- Understand digital signatures

Key Terms

Asymmetric-key encryption an encryption method using a key pair or two keys: a public key and a private key, one to encrypt data and the other to decrypt those data

Authentication token a physical device used to authenticate users

Ciphertext data which cannot be understood without decoding it first

Digital certificate an electronic document that binds a specific asymmetric key pair to the identity of an individual and is issued by a trusted third party; it can be used to distribute the individual's public key to facilitate encrypted communication

Hash encryption a one-way method of encrypting data to produce a unique ciphertext, called a *message digest*; this message digest is fixed length regardless of the size of the original data and cannot be decrypted, but is used instead to prove the integrity of the data

Rainbow table a predefined list of hash values for letters, numbers, and special characters that allows for a time-memory trade-off when trying to match, and therefore crack, a hashed password by comparing the password hash against the table list

Security policy a set of IPSec security settings

Symmetric-key encryption an encryption method using a single key, also called a secret or session key, to both encrypt and decrypt data

Introduction to Authentication, Encryption, and Digital Signatures

When communicating over an open network, such as the Internet, it is important to be able to trust the other party when handling sensitive data. This chapter teaches you several technologies being used to authenticate users and encrypt data, and introduces you to the concept of digital signatures. All of these concepts make it possible to be absolutely certain that the person on the other end of the line is legitimate and that no one tampered with the data during transit.

Authentication

Authentication is any method of verifying an individual's identity, usually using usernames and passwords. It is different from authorization, which is providing individuals access to system objects based on their identity. Every user either chooses a password or is assigned a password, and must keep that password secret to avoid identity theft.

Passwords must be created so they cannot be easily guessed. They should use at least eight characters and include numbers and special characters.

In addition to passwords, sometimes physical *authentication tokens* are used. These devices can be used much like a credit card to log into the network or can present a constantly changing number to authenticate the user. Some authentication tokens can be plugged into computers using USB ports.

RSA SecurID

RSA SecurID provides two-factor authentication based on both something the user knows (a password or PIN) and something the user has (an authenticator). Because it uses two factors, it is more secure than just a simple password. SecurID is useful for authenticating users before they interact with applications through any of the following means:

- VPNs and WLANs
- E-mail
- Intranets and extranets
- Microsoft Windows desktops
- Web servers
- Other network resources

The RSA authentication method has become an industry standard for asset security.

Smart Cards

A smart card is a small card that contains a microprocessor and memory chip. The microprocessor is used to add or delete the information on the memory chip. It can only undertake predefined operations, so it is especially useful for authentication.

VeriSign Authentication

VeriSign Unified Authentication provides a single platform for an organization's strong authentication requirements. Using this platform, security is handled remotely on VeriSign's servers, which allows it to be constantly updated with no action required by end users. Authentication methods include the VeriSign Unified Authentication Multipurpose Next-Generation Token Hybrid and USB Token, the VeriSign One-Time Password (OTP) Token, and the VeriSign Secure Storage Token.

Authenticating Network Clients

On the Internet, once information reaches a firewall, the source must be identified. The firewall determines users' identities using digital signatures, public keys, and private keys that are established by complex algorithms. These methods can also be used to encrypt and decrypt e-mail messages and files.

Encryption

Encryption is the process of converting data into *ciphertext*, which cannot be understood without decoding it first. Reading an encrypted file requires access to a secret key or password that can be used to decrypt it. Due to the public nature of the Internet, it is important to encrypt many types of data when communicating, including:

- Credit card information
- Social Security numbers
- Private correspondence
- Personal details
- Sensitive company information
- Bank account information

There are two main computer encryption systems:

1. Symmetric-key encryption
2. Public-key encryption

Implementing Encryption in Firewalls

Firewalls perform encryption only on certain components. They mainly focus on features such as packet forwarding and NAT (Network Address Translation). Though the firewall protects the system from attacks, executable code can be corrupted before it reaches the firewall, often through malevolent e-mail attachments or HTTP downloads.

Encryption is important in firewalls for the following reasons:

- Protects from attacks
- Preserves data integrity
- Enhances confidentiality
- Allows user authentication
- Enables Virtual Private Network (VPN)

Hackers take advantage of poorly encrypted firewalls by performing both active and passive attacks. Active attacks hijack communication sessions, disabling the server and giving the attacker control of the session. Passive attacks include packet sniffing and programs that scan for open ports to be compromised. Figure 3-1 shows a vulnerable, unencrypted packet, while Figure 3-2 shows an encrypted packet.

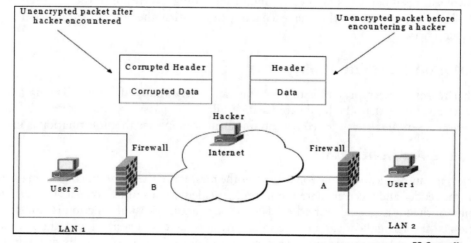

Figure 3-1   This shows an unencrypted packet, intercepted by a hacker.

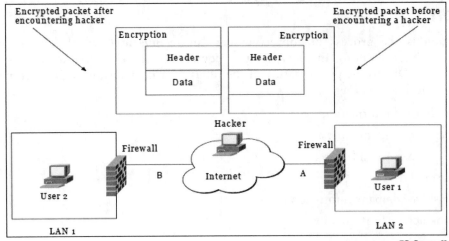

Figure 3-2   This shows an encrypted packet, protected from hackers.

Cost of Firewall Encryption

The primary cost of encryption is CPU time. The bastion host hosts the firewall and performs encryption along with other security functions. Encrypted packets must be padded to a uniform length in order to work with many encryption algorithms, which increases the time needed to process them. Encrypting and decrypting data in the firewall slows down the system, which increases the time it takes to perform other tasks. In addition, the administrator will have to review firewall log files, adding a cost in human time.

Preserving Data Integrity

The main reason to encrypt information is to preserve its integrity. Encrypted packets cannot be meaningfully modified, so they will remain accurate. Still, threats such as man-in-the-middle attacks are possible, where hackers intercept encrypted data sessions to overwrite data. However, most authentication methods will catch this tampering, thus maintaining data integrity.

Along with data integrity, encryption provides nonrepudiation. This protects each participant from the other party denying what took place. Encryption confirms that the electronic transaction occurred, along with who was involved. Each party is supposed to obtain something as a result of the transaction. A digital signature is attached to the files exchanged so that each party can confirm the other's identity, enabling trusted communications over a network.

Maintaining Confidentiality

Another reason to encrypt data is to keep the data secret and confidential. The data in stolen computers are often more valuable than the hardware itself. While many passwords can be cracked with the right software, encryption is very important for confidential information in case that information is intercepted.

Message Authentication

The message authentication function computes the message authentication code from the message and the secret key. If the sender and receiver share the secret key, calculation can be done at the receiving end using the same function of the message and secret key. The message authentication function is similar to cryptographic hash functions. Message authentication code values are generated and verified with the same secret key.

Different secret keys should exist for every pair of users. This is logistically difficult, because the number of keys increases exponentially as more users are added. However, if one secret key is shared among all users, the compromise of one key means the compromise of the whole system.

Strength

The strength of encryption systems generally depends on the cryptographic keys and the mathematical algorithms used. A poorly implemented security technology or weak algorithm is not only easily cracked, but can also leave unintentional backdoors for attackers to find and exploit.

A well-designed cryptographic system is very difficult to break. The keys provided in public-key algorithms are longer than the keys used in symmetric algorithms.

Hashing Algorithms

In public-key encryption, the key is based on a hash value. This value is determined by using a hashing algorithm on the base value. While it is simple to determine the hash value of a set of data, it is impossible to extract the data from the hash value through any means other than brute force and the use of rainbow tables. A *rainbow table* is a predefined list of hash values for letters, numbers, and special characters that allows for a time-memory trade-off when trying to match, and therefore crack, a hashed password by comparing the password hash against the table list. Public keys use complex hash algorithms producing 40-bit or even 128-bit numbers, which would take years to crack using brute-force methods. A 128-bit number has a possible 2^{128}, or 3,402,823,669,209,384, 634,633,746,074,300,000,000,000,000,000,000,000,000,000,000,000, possible combinations.

HMAC

HMAC is one secret-key authentication algorithm. Data integrity and data origin authentication provided by HMAC depend on how widely the secret key is distributed. If the HMAC key is known by only the source and destination, this provides both data integrity and data origin authentication. It can be used with an iterative cryptographic hash function such as MD5 or SHA-1 in combination with the secret shared key. HMAC is stronger when used with stronger hash algorithms.

MD5

MD5 is a block-chained hashing algorithm. The first block is hashed with an initial seed, resulting in a hash. That hash is summed with the seed, and the result becomes the seed for the next block. When the last block is computed, its next-seed value becomes the hash for the entire stream. As a result, blocks cannot be hashed in parallel.

This algorithm takes as input a message of arbitrary length and produces a 128-bit fingerprint or message digest of the input. This algorithm is designed for digital signature applications, where a large file must be compressed in a secure manner before being encrypted with a secret key under a public-key system such as RSA.

Encryption Algorithms

There are several encryption algorithms available, including the following:

- *RSA*: RSA uses a public and private key. Data are divided into blocks, all of the same size, and those blocks are individually encrypted and transferred. Blocks are encrypted using the public key and can then be decrypted only with the corresponding private key.

- *Diffie-Hellman*: This algorithm is used to exchange keys securely between two systems that do not share any common keys. It is notable because if the authentication is ever compromised, previously exchanged data cannot be read.

- *Digital Signature Standard (DSS)*: DSS has been the authentication standard for the U.S. government since its creation by the National Institute of Standards and Technology (NIST) in 1994. Digital signatures are created by private keys and verified by public keys.

- *ElGamal*: ElGamal is similar to Diffie-Hellman, except encrypted messages become twice the size of their plaintext counterparts. This makes it much better suited for small amounts of data.

- *RC2 and RC4*: RC2 is used for DES, including triple encryption. RC4 is used in Secure Sockets Layer (SSL) and Wired Equivalent Privacy (WEP). These have been in existence since 1987 and provide poor security compared to newer algorithms.

- *International Data Encryption Algorithm (IDEA)*: IDEA is used in PGP and SSH. It operates on 64-bit blocks and uses 128-bit keys.

- *Snefru*: Snefru gives a hash code of 128 bits or 256 bits. However, it has known faults that can be exploited.

- *RIPEMD-160*: This newer version of RIPEMD is a 160-bit message digest algorithm.

- *HAVAL*: HAVAL is a faster modification of MD5 that produces hash values from 92 to 256 bits.

- *Skipjack*: This algorithm was developed by the U.S. National Security Agency (NSA), and was a secret algorithm but is now public. It uses an 80-bit key to encrypt and decrypt data in 64-bit blocks.

- *XOR*: Several browsers use XOR, because it is simple and secure. It uses the same key for both encryption and decryption. Keys of any length can be used, but shorter keys are easier to crack.

- *Blowfish*: Blowfish is the standard in OpenBSD and supports keys from 32 bits to 448 bits.

- *Camellia*: This uses the Advanced Encryption Standard (AES) interface, with 128-bit blocks and 128-bit, 192-bit, or 256-bit keys.

- *CAST*: Similar to Blowfish, CAST is a freely available encryption algorithm used for general purposes.

- *Tiny Encryption Algorithm (TEA)*: TEA is one of the fastest and most efficient algorithms, using 64-bit data blocks and 128-bit keys.

- *Size-Changing Algorithms (SCAs)*: SCAs take one stream of input and produce output of differing sizes. This reduces the overall size of the data to save on storage space and transmission bandwidth. They transform the data to make the data even more difficult to decode without the decryption key.

Analyzing Popular Encryption Schemes

Symmetric-Key Encryption Versus Asymmetric-Key Encryption

Symmetric-key encryption is an encryption method using a single key, also called a secret or session key, to both encrypt and decrypt data. In symmetric-key encryption schemes, both parties have separate private keys. These keys must always be kept private. The issue with this is scalability. If an organization has 100 employees, each individual must have 100 separate keys, one for each person. Figure 3-3 shows symmetric-key encryption.

Asymmetric-key encryption is an encryption method using a key pair: a public key and a private key, one to encrypt data and the other to decrypt those data. Only the private keys must be kept secret. These schemes are slower than symmetric key schemes, but fewer keys are required. Figure 3-4 shows asymmetric-key encryption.

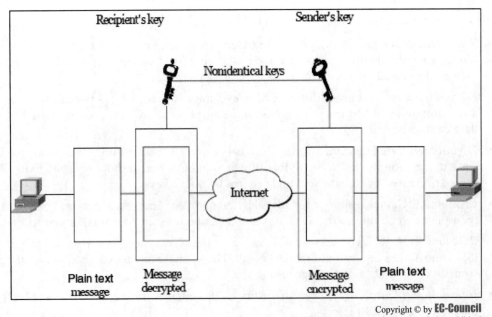

Figure 3-3   Symmetric-key encryption schemes involve private keys for both parties.

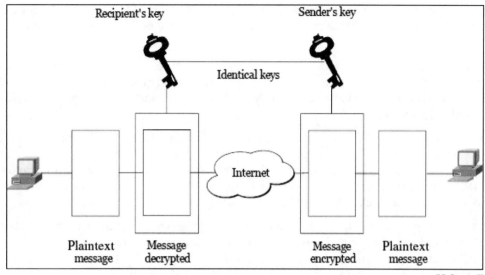

Figure 3-4 Asymmetric-key encryption schemes require both private keys and public keys.

Key Management Protocols (Bundling, Electronic Key, Over-The-Air Rekeying) The main aim of a key management scheme is to provide two communicating devices with a common shared cryptographic key. First, a master key is shared between the devices. That key is used to create session keys.

A Key Management Controller (KMC) can be used to communicate new keys, a process often called rekeying. The KMC will assign keys though Over-the-Air Rekeying (OTAR), which means keys are assigned over radio channels.

Hashing

Hash encryption is a one-way method of encrypting data to produce a unique ciphertext, called a *message digest*. This message digest is fixed length regardless of the size of the original data and cannot be decrypted, but is used instead to prove the integrity of the data. The hash is generated by a formula, and no two texts will produce the same hash value. In security systems, hash values are sent along with messages. Once the recipient decrypts a message, the message is hashed, and if the hash values match, the message was received intact.

Hashing can also be used for accessing data records. For example, consider the following list of names:

- John Smith
- Sarah Jones
- Roger Adams

To create a hash table for these records, the same formula is applied to each name to produce a unique numerical value, which will result in values such as:

- 1345873 John Smith
- 3097905 Sarah Jones
- 4060964 Roger Adams

If the user then wanted to search for Sarah Jones's record, the system would run the hashing formula on "Sarah Jones," which would produce the numerical index key, making it easy for the system to find Sarah's record.

Data Encryption Standard (DES)

DES is the most widely used encryption algorithm. It is usually used as a block cipher, working on 64-bit plaintext blocks and returning ciphertext blocks of the same size using a 56-bit key.

DES has four modes of use: two block modes of encryption (ECB and CBC) and two stream modes of encryption (CFB and OFB). Block modes split the messages into blocks, while stream modes work with a stream of bits.

Electronic Codebook Book (ECB)   Messages are divided into several 64-bit blocks that are encrypted. Repetitions in the message can be reflected in the ciphertext, which is a problem when encrypting media. The main weakness with ECB is that encrypted blocks are independent of one another, so they can be broken individually.

Cipher Block Chaining (CBC)   Messages are divided into 64-bit blocks, but those blocks are connected together. Each ciphertext block is dependent upon all message blocks before it, so changing one block changes all blocks after it. To start, an initial value (IV) is required, which must be known by both sender and receiver. If the IV is sent in the clear, the attacker can intercept it and change it, so the IV should first be encrypted in ECB mode. If the last block is smaller than 64 bits, it must be padded to 64 bits.

Cipher Feedback Mode (CFB)   This mode first uses the Boolean logical process of exclusive OR (XOR) on each plaintext block with the previous ciphertext block, and then the result is encrypted with the DES key. This makes all the blocks dependent on all the previous blocks. This mode of operation emulates a *stream cipher* and is similar to CBC, but it is slower than ECB due to the added complexity.

Output Feedback Mode (OFB)   This is similar to CFB mode, except that the ciphertext output of DES is fed back into an arbitrary initial value that has been passed through the DES algorithm, rather than the actual final ciphertext. This arbitrary initial value is called the *shift register*.

3DES   3DES is a form of DES in which three 64-bit keys are used for an overall key length of 192 bits. The user-provided key is broken into three subkeys, and the data are encrypted by each of the three keys in sequence. It is three times as slow as DES, but also three times as secure.

Pretty Good Privacy (PGP)

PGP is a hybrid system that makes use of both symmetric and asymmetric keys. It can use both systems, providing the speed of symmetric cryptography and the scalability of asymmetric cryptography. It works by following these steps:

1. A random key is generated using symmetric cryptography.
2. The message is encrypted.
3. The session key is encrypted using the public key.
4. The recipient of the encrypted message uses a private key to decode the session key.
5. The session key is used to decode the message or file.

Rivest-Shamir-Adelman (RSA) Encryption   RSA was used in the first versions of PGP. It involves processing two large prime numbers through an algorithm; larger prime numbers give greater security. This must be licensed from RSA Labs.

Diffie-Hellman Encryption   This formula is stronger than RSA. It, too, uses two large numbers that are processed by an algorithm. These two publicly known numbers, of which only one is required to be a prime number, allow two users to interchange a public key over an insecure network such as the Internet.

The Diffie-Hellman implementation of PGP employs two separate keys: a master key and an encryption subkey. One benefit of this system is that a user can generate multiple encryption subkeys based on a single master key. Figure 3-5 shows the creation of subkeys.

X.509

X.509 is a widely accepted, standard set of specifications for collecting and formatting digital certificates and encrypting data within them. Every X.509 implementation utilizes a certificate authority (CA). The CA issues a digital certificate, eliminates the need for an associated public key to be distributed, and guarantees security, because it is issued by a trusted third party.

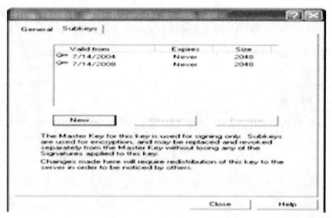

Figure 3-5   Diffie-Hellman encryption allows users to make subkeys based on their master keys.

Because it is the most widely accepted format, it is cross-functional with most of today's public-key infrastructures (PKIs). The structure of an X.509 v3 digital certificate is as follows:

- Version
- Serial number
- Algorithm ID
- Issuer
- Validity
  - Not before
  - Not after
- Subject
- Subject public-key info
  - Public-key algorithm
  - Subject public key
- Issuer unique identifier (optional)
- Subject unique identifier (optional)
- Extensions (optional)
- Certificate signature algorithm
- Certificate signature

Secure Sockets Layer (SSL)

SSL is the standard method of securely transmitting data over the Internet. An SSL session employs both symmetric and asymmetric keys. The asymmetric keys are used to start an SSL session, but symmetric keys are dynamically produced during data transfer.

An SSL data transaction occurs over the following steps:

1. Clients connect to a Web server using the SSL protocol.
2. The two machines organize a handshake, through which they can verify each other's identity and agree on what formulas and protocols will be used to encrypt and exchange information. The client sends the server its preferences for cipher settings, the SSL version number, and a randomly generated number to be used in the future.

3. The server responds with an SSL version number and its own cipher preferences, including its digital signatures. The digital certificate includes the issuer's identity, a date range, and the public key of the server.

4. The client verifies that the data and other information on the digital certificate are authentic. The domain name on the digital certificate is verified against the domain name of the server. If it matches, the client generates a pre–master code and sends it to the server using the server's public key. The client's digital certificate is also transmitted if it is requested by the server.

5. The server uses its private key to decrypt the pre–master code sent by the client. The server generates the master secret that will be used by both the client and server to generate session keys.

6. The session keys are generated and used to encrypt data transmitted between the client and the server.

IPSec

Firewalls can generate virtual private networks (VPNs) using IPSec. This creates a trusted IP connection between two systems, running under the application layer, transparent to the user. IPSec allows a computer to automatically protect e-mail, Web traffic, and file transfers. If a user installs a firewall that supports encryption, it is likely that the user uses IPSec.

IPSec can be executed on Windows XP/2000 and above, Linux, and Mac OS. IPSec standards support IPv6, the latest version of IP that supports 128-bit addressing. IPSec ensures data integrity and confidentiality by authenticating the source of data packets. Two computers implementing IPSec can authenticate each other when a connection is established between them. Data can still be transferred to other machines that do not implement IPSec if the other machine is in tunnel mode.

Figure 3-6 shows the IPSec architecture.

IPSec Protocols

IPSec has two protocols: Authentication Header (AH) and Encapsulating Security Payload (ESP).

Authentication Header (AH)

AH adds a digital signature to the data packets in order to secure them from attacks such as spoofing and tampering. It checks the packet headers to detect if the source and destination IP addresses are changed, and rejects them if they are. The digital signature and authentication headers are added to the TCP/IP packet. These headers save information in the following order:

1. IP header
2. Authentication header
3. TCP header
4. Digital signature
5. Data

AH is not compatible with NAT, because the changes in IP addresses cause the packets to be rejected.

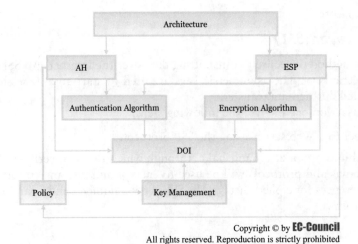

Figure 3-6   This is the architecture of IPSec.

Encapsulating Security Payload (ESP)

The ESP protocol is stronger than the AH protocol because it encrypts the IP packet's data payload. Data are stored between the ESP header and the ESP trailer, increasing security.

This mode is also difficult to use with NAT. ESP hides port number information in the packet headers in transport mode. NAT considers such changes a protocol violation and rejects the packets.

ESP hides the TCP/IP header information in the packets in tunnel mode. If IPSec uses the ESP protocol and the firewall uses static Network Address Port Translation (NAPT), the data packets can pass through the network without being rejected. In this case, the information that is translated is the IP address information. Because the connection is already established with the remote host, the packets in which the IP address is hidden are forwarded through the NATP device even though the connection is established through the handshake method.

To use ESP in tunnel mode with a VPN device and a firewall using NAT, the client VPN should use static NAPT.

IPSec Implementation

IPSec can be implemented in the end hosts, routers, or both, based on the user's security requirements.

Host Implementation

In this case, a host is defined as the device from which a packet is originating. Host implementation has the following advantages:

- Provides end-to-end security
- Can implement all modes of IPSec security
- Provides security on a per-flow basis
- Can maintain user context for authentication in establishing IPSec connections

Host implementation can either be integrated into the operating system or between the network layer and data-link layer of the protocol stack (known as "bump in the stack" implementation).

Operating System Integration   If IPSec is integrated into the operating system, it is implemented as part of the network layer. IP stack layering in this case is as follows:

1. Application
2. Transport
3. Network and IPSec
4. Data link

Integrating IPSec with the OS has the following advantages:

- Because IPSec is strongly integrated into the network layer, it can use network services such as fragmentation, PMTU, and sockets, increasing efficiency.
- It is easy to provide security services per data flow transaction, because key management, the base IPSec protocols, and the network layer can be integrated seamlessly.
- All IPSec modes are supported.

Bump in the Stack (BITS)   If OS integration is impossible, bump-in-the-stack implementation is the only option. Using BITS, IP stack layering is as follows:

1. Application
2. Transport
3. Network
4. IPSec
5. Data link

This implementation's major issue is the duplication of efforts. It becomes very difficult to handle issues such as fragmentation, PMTU, and routing. On the other hand, it does have the capability to provide a complete solution because of the piecemeal implementation of the IPSec protocol between OSI layers, rather than at the network layer where it was designed to function.

Router Implementation

Implementing IPSec at the router has the following advantages:

- It has the capability to secure packets flowing between two networks over a public network such as the Internet.
- It has the ability to authenticate and authorize users to enter into the private network. This is used by many organizations to allow their employees to communicate over the Internet using a VPN.

There are two types of router implementations: native implementation and bump in the wire (BITW).

Native Implementation   This is similar to OS-integrated implementation on the hosts. In this implementation, IPSec is integrated with the router software, as shown in Figure 3-7.

Bump in the Wire (BITW)   This is similar to the BITS implementation. Here, IPSec is implemented in a device that is connected to the physical interface of the router. This device usually does not run any routing algorithm but is used only to secure packets. This is not a viable long-term solution, because it is not possible to have a device attached to every interface of the router. Figure 3-8 shows BITW implementation.

IPSec Components

IPSec has the following components:

- *IPSec driver*: This is the software that performs protocol-level functions required to encrypt, decrypt, authenticate, and verify the packets.
- *Internet Key Exchange (IKE)*: IKE is the IPSec protocol that produces security keys for IPSec and other protocols.
- *Internet Security Association Key Management Protocol (ISAKMP)*: ISAKMP is an IPSec protocol that allows two computers to communicate by encrypting data using common security settings. It also secures the exchange of keys.
- *Oakley*: Oakley is a protocol that uses the Diffie-Hellman algorithm to create a master key and a key that is specific to each session in IPSec data transfer.
- *IPSec Policy Agent*: This is a service of Windows 2000 that collects IPSec policy settings from Active Directory and sets the configuration at startup.

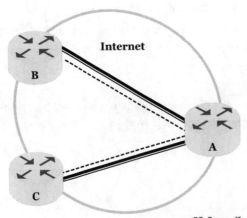

Figure 3-7   This is the native implementation of IPSec on a router.

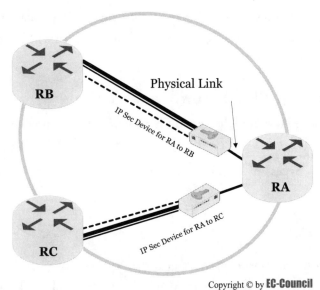

Figure 3-8   This is the bump-in-the-wire implementation
of IPSec on a router.

IPSec Modes

IPSec has two modes, chosen in the security policy: transport mode and tunnel mode. The mode is chosen based on whether or not the network uses network address translation (NAT). Networks using NAT can only use transport mode, where IPSec is used to authenticate two hosts connected for data transfer, with the option to encrypt the transferred data. In tunnel mode, IPSec encapsulates the data packets and encrypts packet headers but not the actual data. A firewall will assume these packets are invalid and reject them.

Because there are two protocols and two modes, there are four different combinations of protocol and mode, and each combination has a different use:

- ESP in transport mode is useful when data integrity and privacy are needed in a network and a VPN is not used.

- AH in transport mode is useful when data integrity is needed but confidentiality is not a concern.

- ESP in tunnel mode is useful when data integrity and privacy are needed, the firewall does not use NAT, and the network uses a VPN. This mode provides the highest level of security because ESP hides IP header information, and tunnel mode encapsulates and encrypts packets.

- AH in tunnel mode is useful when the firewall uses NAT and the network uses a VPN.

IPSec Configuration

IPSec is implemented in Windows 2000 and above as an administrative tool used to enforce security policies on IP network traffic. IPSec filters are inserted into the IP layer of the TCP/IP networking protocol stack to check all inbound or outbound IP packets.

A *security policy* is a set of IPSec security settings. Windows 2000 and above provide a graphical user interface and different command-line tools that can be used to configure a security policy and then assign it to a computer.

Enabling IPSec

If the security policy specifies the use of IPSec, the network administrator has to choose a group policy setting for all the computers that require security. During the initiation of a session between computers that use IPSec, the following takes place:

1. ISAKMP collects the policy settings of the computers.

2. ISAKMP compares, collects, and creates a security association (SA) between them, depending on their policy settings.

3. The Oakley protocol creates a master key, which secures the IPSec data transfer.

4. Depending on the session's security policy, the IPSec driver verifies, filters, and protects the transport layer from network traffic.

Internet Key Exchange (IKE) Security Associations

The IKE protocol is designed to secure the relationship between two computers, negotiate security options, and dynamically generate shared secret cryptographic keys. The security association (SA) is the agreement between the security setting and the keys.

IKE negotiates two types of security associations: main-mode security associations and IPSec security associations.

IPSec Processing Steps

1. A consumer sends a message to a service provider.

2. The consumer's IPSec driver attempts to match the outgoing packet's address or type against the IP filter.

3. The IPSec driver instructs ISAKMP to initiate security negotiations with the service provider.

4. The service provider's ISAKMP receives the security negotiations request.

5. Both principals initiate a key exchange, establishing an ISAKMP SA and a shared secret key.

6. Both principals negotiate the security level for the information exchange, establishing both IPSec SAs and keys.

7. The consumer's IPSec driver transfers packets to the appropriate connection type for transmission to the service provider.

8. The provider receives the packets and transfers them to the IPSec driver.

9. The provider's IPSec uses the inbound SA and key to check the digital signature and begin decryption.

10. The provider's IPSec driver transfers decrypted packets to the OSI transport layer for further processing.

IPSec Algorithms

IPSec uses two authentication algorithms and several encryption algorithms. The authentication algorithms, HMAC-MD5 and HMAC-SHA1, both use secret keys generated by ISAKMP/Oakley. The following are some encryption algorithms that may be used:

- DES (used in ESP)
- CAST (RFC 2144)
- RC5 (RFC 2040)
- IDEA
- Blowfish

IPSec Policies

The IPSec policy is a set of rules that governs when the IPSec protocol should be used. This policy directly communicates with the IPSec driver. When using Windows Server, IPSec policy should be defined at the group level, while it should be defined at the local policy level for desktop operating systems. The following are the predefined IPSec policy levels in Windows operating systems:

- *Client (Respond Only)*: The client does not start communication using IPSec on its own, but it will participate when other systems require it.

- *Server (Request Security)*: The host will request to use IPSec, but will still communicate with a client that does not use it.

- *Secure Server (Require Security)*: The host will only communicate with clients who use IPSec. When the security level increases, network performance decreases.

The following are the parts of the IPSec policy:

- *IP filters*: This is a list that instructs IPSec which inbound and outbound traffic should be secured based on IP address, port number, and protocol.

- *Filter action*: Filter action tells the policy agent how items on the IP filter list should be secured.

- *Authentication methods*: Authentication methods are security algorithms that are used for key exchange and authentication.

- *Tunnel setting*: IPSec tunnel setting includes the IP address or DNS name of the destination PC.

- *Connection type*: This variable tells IPSec whether it is being used across a LAN or a WAN.

IPSec Limitations

IPSec has the following limitations:

- If a computer using IPSec is compromised, all communications from that machine cannot be trusted, including the IPSec protocol.

- An IP connection is encrypted, but not the message content. The text of e-mails cannot be encrypted or secured.

- Source and destination data security is not provided by IPSec.

- IPSec is used to validate computers, but it does not secure the users. Even the use of a digital certificate with data transfer does not authenticate the user.

- IPSec does not restrict users from viewing and modifying the contents of packets and permits intruders to identify information such as source and destination IP addresses and packet sizes.

Digital Certificates

A *digital certificate* is an electronic document that binds a specific asymmetric key pair to the identity of an individual, and is issued by a trusted third party. It can be used to distribute the individual's public key to facilitate encrypted communication. This certificate acts much like a driver's license, passport, or membership card. Users and organizations can present these digital certificates electronically to prove their identities in order to access information or online services. Digital certificates follow the X.509 standard to provide a complete security solution and ensure the identity of all users involved in online transactions.

Digital certificates are issued by a certificate authority (CA) and signed with a private key. A digital certificate generally contains the following:

- Details of owner's public key
- Owner's name
- Expiration date of public key
- Name of the certificate authority (CA) that issued the digital certificate
- Serial number of the digital signature
- Digital signature of the issuing CA

Standards for Digital Certificates

Important standards for digital certificates include:

- Secure Sockets Layer (SSL)
- Secure/Multipurpose Internet Mail Extensions (S/MIME)

- Secure Electronic Transaction (SET)
- Internet Protocol Security (IPSec)

X.509 as Authentication Standard

X.509 is an authentication standard commonly used by public-key certificates. It uses two different levels of authentication: simple authentication is based on use of a password to verify user identity, and strong authentication uses credentials created by cryptographic methods. Digital certificates require strong authentication. Public-key cryptography is used for strong authentication, and while X.509 does not depend on one particular cryptographic algorithm, two users wishing to authenticate one another must support the same algorithm.

Public-Key Certificate

A public-key certificate is a digitally signed document that authenticates the sender's identity. It contains a specially formatted block of data that includes the name of the certificate holder, the public key of that holder, and the digital signature of a certification authority. The certification authority verifies that the details in the certificate are correct and associated with the sender's name and the public key in the document. A user ID packet with the sender's unique identifier is sent after the certificate packet. A public-key certificate has different functions such as authorization for a specific action or delegation of authority. Public-key certificates are part of a public-key infrastructure that deals with digitally signed documents.

Viewing Digital Certificates

Certificates usually contain a large amount of information. There are a few relatively simple steps to be taken to ensure that the certificate is valid—for example, checking to see if it was issued by a reputable organization, checking whether the person to whom the certificate was issued can be trusted, and checking whether the certificate was used while it was valid.

To view certificates for a file, a user can follow these steps:

1. From the Tools menu in Internet Explorer, choose **Internet Options**.
2. Click the **Content** tab.
3. Click **Certificates**.
4. To view details about a particular certificate, select the name of the signer, and then click **View Certificate**.

If macro security is set to medium or high, a warning will appear before opening files that contain macros signed with suspicious certificates. Users can click **Details** in the warning dialog box to view the properties of the certificate.

To view certificates for a file that is already open, a user can follow these steps:

1. On the Tools menu, choose **Macro**, and then choose **Visual Basic Editor**.
2. Use the Project Explorer to select the desired macro project.
3. In the Visual Basic Editor, choose **Digital Signature** from the Tools menu.
4. In the **Digital Signature** dialog box, click **Detail** to view the details of the certificate.

Digital Signatures

Digital signatures supported by public-key infrastructures are the most effective way to ensure digital verification for electronic transactions. A digital signature is similar to a handwritten signature and has the following properties:

- With the help of the digital signature author, the date and time of the signature can be verified.
- Authentication of content is possible at the time the content was signed.
- It can be verified by a third party in case of disputes.

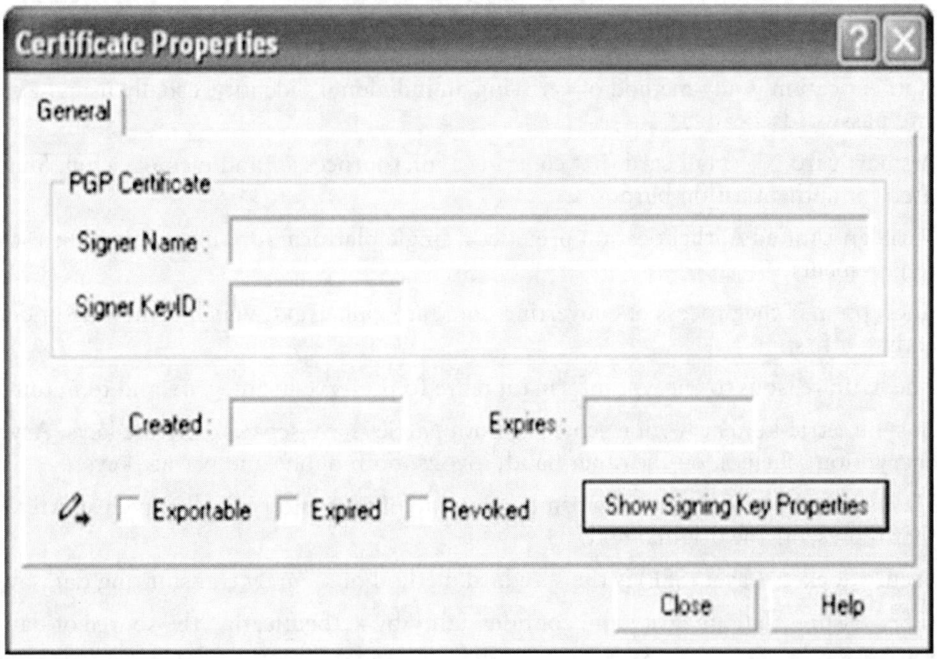

Figure 3-9 Digital certificates include a name, an ID, a creation date, and an expiration date.

Digital standards are open and internationally recognized. They make it very clear to the recipient if data were altered during transmission.

The majority of organizations use a Lightweight Directory Access Protocol (LDAP) directory that possesses publicly available information about digital certificates, as well as individual users in the organization and organization's network.

There are two types of digital certificates: client-based and server-based. Client-based digital certificates are obtained by an individual user from a certificate authority (CA), while server-based digital certificates are issued by a CA to a company, which then issues them to individuals.

Figure 3-9 shows the basic information associated with a digital signature.

Private-Key Infrastructure (PKI)

The primary use of PKI is to allow distribution and use of public keys and certificates with security and integrity. Security mechanisms based on PKI include e-mail, e-commerce, home banking, and electronic postal systems.

PKI enables basic security services for varied systems using the following:

- SSL, IPSec, and HTTPS for communication and transactional security
- S/MIME and PGP for e-mail security
- SET for value exchange
- Identrus for B2B

The following are some key benefits of PKI:

- Reduces transactional processing expenses
- Reduces risk
- Improves efficiency and performance of systems and networks
- Reduces the difficulty of security systems with binary symmetrical methods

Chapter Summary

- Authentication is any method of verifying an individual's identity, usually using usernames and passwords.

- A smart card is a small card that contains a microprocessor and memory chip. Smart cards are often used for authentication purposes.

- VeriSign Unified Authentication provides a single platform for an organization's strong authentication requirements.

- Encryption is the process of converting data into ciphertext, which cannot be understood without decoding it first.

- The main reasons to encrypt information are to preserve its integrity and to maintain confidentiality.

- In symmetric-key encryption schemes, both parties have separate private keys. Asymmetric-key encryption schemes, on the other hand, involve both public and private keys.

- Hashing is the process of transforming a string of text into typically much shorter, fixed-length value that represents the original text.

- Secure Sockets Layer (SSL) is the standard method of securely transmitting data over the Internet.

- IPSec ensures data integrity and confidentiality by authenticating the source of data packets.

- IPSec has two protocols: Authentication Header (AH) and Encapsulating Security Payload (ESP). IPSec has two modes, chosen in the security policy: transport mode and tunnel mode.

- A digital certificate is an electronic document that provides credential information for online transactions.

- Digital signatures supported by public-key infrastructures are the most effective way to ensure digital verification for electronic transactions.

Review Questions

1. What are authentication tokens?

2. What is VeriSign Unified Authentication?

3. What is encryption?

4. What is IDEA?

5. What are symmetric- and asymmetric-key encryptions?

_____

_____

_____

_____

6. What is PGP?

_____

_____

_____

_____

7. What are the steps in an SSL data transaction?

_____

_____

_____

_____

8. What are the components of IPSec?

_____

_____

_____

_____

9. What are the modes of IPSec?

_____

_____

_____

_____

10. What are some limitations of IPSec?

_____

_____

_____

_____

11. What are digital certificates?

_____

_____

_____

_____

12. What are the functions of PKI?

_____

_____

_____

_____

Hands-On Projects

1. Use Encrypt My Folder to lock files and folders with a personal password.

   - Navigate to Chapter 3 of the Student Resource Center.
   - Install and launch the Encrypt My Folder program.
   - Select the file or folder to be protected.
   - Click **Password** to open the **Password** window.
   - Type the password in the **Password** and **Confirm Password** fields and click **OK**.
   - A notice window is displayed to indicate that the password was successfully set. Click **OK**.
   - Select the file or folder to be locked.
   - Click **LOCK** to lock the file or folder.
   - A notice window is displayed to indicate that the file or folder was successfully locked. Click **OK**.
   - Select the file or folder to be unlocked.
   - Click **UNLOCK** to unlock the file or folder.
   - A notice window is displayed to indicate that the file or folder was successfully unlocked. Click **OK**.
   - Click **SETTINGS** to open the **Settings** window. Click **OK**.
   - Click **QUIT** to exit the application.

2. Use SafeCryptor for safe, fast, and reliable text encryption.

   - Navigate to Chapter 3 of the Student Resource Center.
   - Install and launch the SafeCryptor program.
   - Type the text to be encrypted in the text field.
   - Click the certificate icon to obtain the system's unique key.
   - Click **Encrypt** to encrypt the text.
   - Click **Decrypt** to retrieve the plaintext.

3. Use EncryptOnClick to encrypt and decrypt files.

   - Navigate to Chapter 3 of the Student Resource Center.
   - Install and launch the EncryptOnClick program.
   - In the **Encrypt** pane, click **File** and select the file or folder to be encrypted.
   - In the **Password** window, type the password in the **Password** and **Confirm Password** fields. his will encrypt the file or folder.
   - In the **Decrypt** pane, click **File** and select the file or folder to be decrypted.
   - Type the password in the **Password** field and click **OK**. This will decrypt the file or folder.
   - Click **Close** to exit the application.

4. Use CrypSecure to encrypt sensitive data on your computer.

   - Navigate to Chapter 3 of the Student Resource Center.
   - Install and launch the CrypSecure program.
   - Click **Files and Folders**, browse the location of the file to encrypt, and click **Encrypt**.
   - Browse to an encrypted file and click **Decrypt** to decrypt the file.
   - Click **Close** in the **Files and Folders** window.
   - Click **Close** to close the window.

5. Use CryptoHeaven to send encrypted e-mail and securely back up and share files.

- Navigate to Chapter 3 of the Student Resource Center.
- Install and launch the CryptoHeaven program.
- When the **Login** window appears, click **New Account**.
- Fill in the details and select **Server**.
- Select **Create**.
- An e-mail will arrive providing information for creating a new account. Follow the link in this e-mail.
- Type the **Login** and **Password** information and click **Login**.
- Click **eMail Folders**.
- Click **New Mail**.
- Select the recipients.
- Type the message.
- Click **Send your secure E-mail**.
- Click **File Upload**, select a file to be uploaded, and click **OK**.
- Click **Upload**.
- Click **Exit**.

Chapter 4

Virtual Private Networks

Objectives

After completing this chapter, you should be able to:

- Identify the functional types of VPNs
- Understand and implement tunneling protocols
- Implement VPN security
- Set up a VPN
- Implement VPN servers
- Configure DHCP, IAS, and VPN servers
- Identify VPN policies with registrations and passwords
- Troubleshoot risks associated with VPNs
- Understand VPN product testing

Key Terms

Internet Engineering Task Force (IETF)   a large, open, international community of network designers, operators, vendors, and researchers concerned with the evolution of the Internet architecture and the smooth operation of the Internet by developing and promoting Internet standards

Multihomed host   a host computer having more than one network connection or having multiple IP addresses assigned to one network interface card (NIC)

Network access server (NAS)   a gateway server that provides a single point of access to remote resources such as Internet Web sites

Point of presence (POP) server   an access point provided by the ISP to the Internet

Split tunneling   a tunneling method that allows a VPN user to access both a public network and a local area network at the same time, using the same physical network interface

Introduction to Virtual Private Networks

The Internet provides an easy and cost-effective way to communicate, but its open nature poses a severe security problem. Virtual private networks, or VPNs, allow secure connectivity over unsecure networks, including the Internet. Tunneling protocols employed by VPNs help to achieve encryption, data integrity, and authentication. This chapter will teach you the basics of VPNs, including how they work and how to implement them.

VPN Classification

There are several types of VPNs, including internal LAN VPNs, remote access VPNs, and extranet VPNs.

Internal LAN VPNs

Internal LAN VPNs establish connections between the branches of one organization through the Internet. Each department has a gateway installed, which serves as a firewall to secure the LAN. The VPN encrypts data sent to the user, but the data sent through the Internet are not encrypted by the VPN. Figure 4-1 is a diagram of an internal LAN VPN.

Remote Access VPNs

Remote access VPNs establish connections between remote clients and a central LAN through the Internet. The VPN software on the client's machine encrypts data packets that are then forwarded to the central LAN. The gateway at the central LAN can close the connection to the VPN after the transfer is complete.

IPSec is the algorithm most commonly used in VPN connections. It includes both key management and encryption methods. Figure 4-2 shows a remote access VPNs.

Extranet VPNs

An extranet VPN establishes a connection between customers and suppliers over the Internet to selected parts of the central intranet. Extranet VPN connections may be temporary or permanent. IPSec is also the standard for extranet VPNs, and all clients and servers should be using IPSec to ensure interoperability. Figure 4-3 shows an extranet VPN.

Tunneling

VPNs use a mechanism called tunneling, which is a virtual connection between the source and destination. This involves encapsulating data packets using a security protocol in order to make them impossible to read if intercepted.

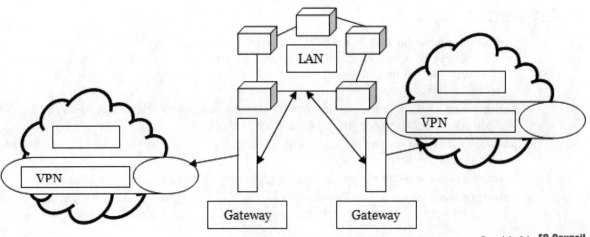

Figure 4-1   Internal LAN VPNs connect two branches of a single organization over the Internet.

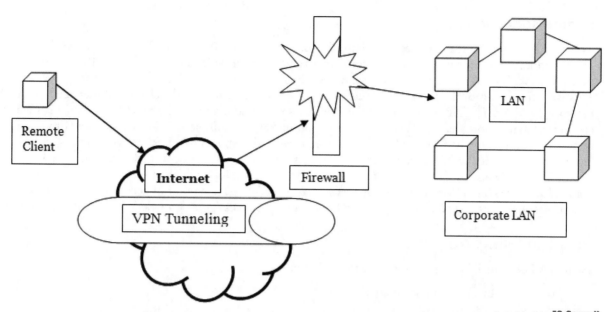

Figure 4-2   A remote access VPN securely connects remote clients to a central LAN.

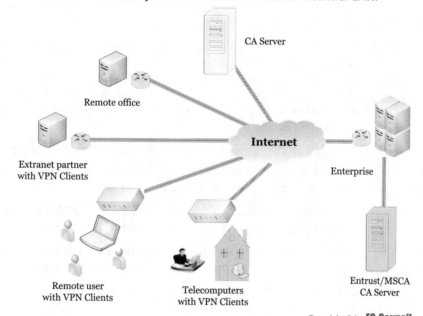

Figure 4-3   An extranet VPN connects customers to selected parts of the central intranet.

Tunneling is not achieved using a fixed line. It uses robust connections to connect to Web sites, and encrypts and encapsulates the IPs for routing, bridging, and filtering packets, similar to wide area networks (WANs). It establishes and maintains a consistent network connection.

Packets created using a specific VPN protocol format are encapsulated inside another base or carrier protocol. VPN protocols help to maintain the integrity and authenticity of information transmitted over the Internet.

Types of Tunneling

There are two types of VPN tunneling: voluntary tunneling and compulsory tunneling.

Voluntary Tunneling

In voluntary tunneling, a connection is established when the VPN client applies for a connection. The VPN client establishes an online connection between the client and the server.

Compulsory Tunneling

Compulsory tunneling is a two-stage configuration of establishing connections. The ISP or network provider sets up the connection for the VPN. If a client connects to a network provider, the provider breaks the normal connection and server logic is built into the VPN server, which acts as a broker device to negotiate the secure connection. This way, the details of the VPN server's connectivity are concealed from the client and managed by the ISP or network provider. The ISPs or the network providers set up and maintain the *multihomed host* system (a host computer having more than one network connection or having multiple IP addresses assigned to one network interface card) to support front-end end processors (FEPs), transport providers, network access servers (NAS), and point of presence (POP) servers. Each FEP has its own network protocol stack, and each is connected to a different TCP/IP network or to different portions of the same network, which in turn connects to the Internet. A *network access server (NAS)* is a gateway server that provides a single point of access to remote resources such as Internet Web sites. A *point of presence (POP) server* is an access point provided by the ISP to the Internet.

VPN Tunneling Protocols

Popular VPN tunneling protocols include the following:

- Point-to-Point Tunneling Protocol (PPTP)
- Layer Two Tunneling Protocol (L2TP)
- Internet Protocol Security (IPSec)

Point-To-Point Tunneling Protocol (PPTP)

PPTP is based on PPP (Point-to-Point Protocol), the standard for connecting networks through dial-up. PPTP works in the second layer of the OSI network model.

PPTP encapsulates data using PPP and then inserts IP datagrams and transmits them through VPN tunnels connected to the Internet. PPTP also encrypts and compresses the packets. Data are transferred using PPTP in GRE (General Routing Encapsulation) form.

VPN tunnels are created in two ways:

1. PPTP users connect to ISPs with PPP using a dial-up modem or ISDN networking.
2. The VPN client and VPN server are connected with a PPTP control connection over broadband using a broker device. TCP port 1723 is used to make these connections.

VPNs can also be connected to the Internet through LANs. In this case, PPTP does not make use of the ISPs, but instead uses a broker device. Using PPTP, data flow through the VPN tunnels in two ways:

1. Information flow is regulated using control messages. The connection to the VPN is established and disconnected with control messages, which are sent between the VPN client and the VPN server.
2. Data packets are transferred between the VPN client and the VPN server.

PPTP Control Connection   After the TCP connection is established, PPTP uses a series of control messages to maintain VPN connections, shown in Table 4-1.

PPTP Security   PPTP is popular particularly because of its security features. Authentication in PPTP is based on PPP protocols such as EAP, CHAP, and PAP. First, the remote client is authenticated, and user access is granted through a trusted domain. Only the user accounts specified in the server's database are given access to the network. Security is assured through secure passwords.

The data traffic is encrypted when it is transferred across the network. When data are transmitted through tunnels, the data are not visible to the rest of the network, and thus they are hidden from hackers. IP, IPX, and NetBEUI packets are all encrypted when using PPTP.

PPTP's authentication protocols support packet filtering, which increases network performance and server reliability. When packet filtering is enabled in a network, it can only accept and send packets that are from authenticated clients, and it rejects packets from unauthorized users.

The major problem with PPTP is that there is no single standard for authentication and encryption. Two different applications that use PPTP may not be compatible with each other if they use different methods of encryption.

Message	Function
StartControlConnectionRequest	Initiates setup of the VPN session, sent by either the client or server
StartControlConnectionReply	Sent as an acknowledgment to the start connection request, indicates the success or failure of the connection as well as the protocol version number
StopControlConnectionReply	An acknowledgment sent to the stop connection request to close the operation based on the result code that indicates the success or failure of the operation
EchoRequestSent	Sent periodically by either client or server to keep the connection alive
EchoReply	Sent in response to the echo request to keep the connection active
OutgoingCallRequest	Creates a VPN tunnel, sent by the client
OutgoingCallReply	Response to the call request containing a unique identifier for that tunnel
IncomingCallRequest	Sent from the client to receive an incoming call from the server
IncomingCallReply	Response to the incoming call request indicating whether the incoming call should be answered
IncomingCallConnected	Response to the incoming call reply providing additional call parameters to the VPN server
CallClearRequest	Sent from the server to a client to disconnect either an incoming or outgoing call
CallDisconnectNotify	Sent from the client to the server in response to the disconnect request
WANErrorNotify	Notification periodically sent to the server containing any CRC, framing, hardware, buffer overrun, timeout, and byte alignment errors
SetLinkInfo	Notifies of any changes to the underlying PPP options

Table 4-1 PPTP uses these control messages to maintain VPN connections

Layer Two Tunneling Protocol (L2TP)

Layer Two Tunneling Protocol (L2TP) is a frequently used tunneling protocol with the following characteristics:

- L2TP is based on the PPTP and L2F protocols. It is the current *Internet Engineering Task Force (IETF)* standard. IETF is a large, open, international community of network designers, operators, vendors, and researchers concerned with the evolution of the Internet architecture and the smooth operation of the Internet by developing and promoting Internet standards.

- Clients accessing the network remotely behave as if they are locally accessing the network. They can access all the same resources as local clients.

- Gateway and access restrictions are shared between remote and local clients.

- Remote clients can only connect to the corporate network.

- There is no need to use special firewalls.

- L2TP is used in tunneling PPP network traffic. This allows remote clients to access the corporate network when in another network.

- Data traffic is first enveloped in virtual PPP and is then tunneled using L2TP.

- IPSec and L2TP can be used together for increased security.

- PPP is used to create dial-up connections. PPP's authentication methods (PAP and CHAP) are used for access control user verification.

- L2TP uses NCP (Network Control Protocol) to assign IP addresses.

- L2TP manages the tunneling of the data-link layer. A dial-up connection from an IP address can be diverted, enabling access to the Internet.

- L2TP can be used for dial-up tunneling in two ways:

  - IP addresses can be dynamically allocated from a pool of addresses in the ISP. Using this method, users have limited access to the organization's network due to firewalls, gateways, and security policies.

  - L2TP can also exist behind corporate firewalls. Behind firewalls, IP addresses are allocated internally, which makes the remote client appear as if it were accessing the connection locally.

L2TP Compulsory Tunnel   An L2TP compulsory tunnel does not require any action on the client side. The ISP has to offer the L2TP Access Concentrator (LAC) function, and the company network has to present the required network and access information to the ISP. In compulsory tunneling, a tunnel is produced without giving the client any alternative. The client sends PPP packets to the ISP's network access server (NAS)/LAC, which wraps them in L2TP and passes them to the LNS (L2TP Network Server).

The ISP creates the L2TP tunnel. The user then dials in to the ISP and creates a PPP session linking the NAS, which responds to the call and creates the virtual PPP tunnel. The NAS then informs the user's home network entryway, located on the other end of the virtual PPP tunnel.

The NAS sends the client's username and password. If the user is legitimate, the NAS and the home entryway set up the tunnel and allocate a session ID linking the user to its tunnel. After the user has been validated and the tunnel has been set up, the client and the home entryway initiate the PPP session, establishing protocols and allotting network addresses to the client.

The user transmits PPP packets to the NAS, which will wrap them in L2TP and send them to the home gateway. When the client sets up the PPP link to the ISP, the ISP allocates an IP address to the client based on the information stored in the LAC database. This IP address applies to the company's network, so it is not a global routable address. The client has no direct authorization to use the Internet. The client appears to be locally associated to the company's network, with all the access and security privileges associated with being a local user.

L2TP Voluntary Tunnel   In voluntary tunneling, the client produces a tunnel using L2TP tunneling software. The user sends L2TP packets to the NAS, which then sends them to the LNS. In voluntary tunneling, the NAS does not need to maintain L2TP, and the LAC exists on the remote client.

In this mode, an L2TP-enabled client sets up a PPP session to an ISP. The ISP allocates a universally routable IP address to the client. The client then introduces an L2TP session directly to its company gateway, without any contribution from the ISP. The client must first set up an L2TP tunnel with its company gateway using a universal IP address. After the L2TP tunnel has been recognized, the client and the company gateway grant the virtual PPP session, setting up protocols and allotting network addresses with hosts on the corporate network.

In this model, the client execution is more complex but it offers more flexibility. It facilitates multiple accesses and removes the need to set up protected tunnels with ISPs and company gateways.

The client can have multiple tunnels to different networks. The client can have more than one IP address assigned to it, for example, the universal routable IP address and the virtual PPP endpoint address. Because the client has a universal routable address, it can still use the Internet. Thanks to the internal company network IP address (virtual PPP endpoint), the client also appears as locally associated to the company network.

Because voluntary tunnels do not involve any setup on the part of the ISP, they are very useful for remote clients who travel. Any ISP point of presence (POP) can be used to link to the corporate network.

VPN Security

VPN provides the following:

- Client privacy
- Data reliability
- Information authenticity

Client Privacy

VPN uses hashing to ensure the confidentiality of data packets. The hash function contains a signature of predefined length, made up of a string of binary numbers. This signature indicates the number of packets sent to the receiver. The information is encrypted and can be decrypted only with that signature, which is only shared between authorized persons. The receiver matches the received signature with the original one to verify its genuineness.

Data Reliability

Security policies employed by the VPN, such as IPSec, protect data from threats and attacks on its resources. Still, VPN connections cannot ensure total end-to-end security, so additional measures should be taken.

Information Authenticity

VPNs are secured using the SSH and IPSec protocols. The integrity of data can be checked with a hash function at the receiving end. If the data are altered in any way, it will be apparent after examining the hash value.

VPN software can be employed to produce and manage tunnels between two security gateways, or between a remote user and a security gateway. These applications cannot manage heavy traffic, but they can share resources and connect to servers. A number of software solutions are available and can be used by managers who wish to employ VPN features, although as new features are included, complexity increases.

It is easier to install and use VPN devices than it is to arrange firewalls, gateways, or routers. Enterprises that cannot afford to install the firewalls can integrate VPN functions, which provide similar services.

VPN Connection

SSH and PPP

There are several advantages to setting up a PPP-SSH VPN. For one, it is generally simpler than other types. PPP and SSH are built into most Linux distributions, and most kernels are preconfigured for their use. If the SSH protocol successfully crosses the firewall, then PPP over SSH will cross the firewall as well. PPP-SSH VPNs do not have any problems with dynamic IP addresses.

There is no problem while mounting VPN over a dial-up connection and connecting multiple tunnels to a single computer; however, the user must ensure that the IP address for each tunnel's network interface is discrete. Both the client and server have PPP daemons that will communicate through the SSH connection.

Concentrator

The concentrator is the server mechanism that validates and allows connections from VPN peers. Remote clients that connect to a VPN using encrypted tunnels connect to the concentrator. It guards the information flow over the Internet. Users can access Web sites or other networks remotely using the concentrator.

There are various models of concentrators available based on the number of clients and bandwidth required. They can encrypt WLAN or wired traffic. The concentrator reduces the operating cost of VPN administration and encryption from gateways and local hosts.

To use a concentrator, a user follows these steps:

1. Configure the network connection.
2. Configure the concentrator.
3. Add users who access the Internet via a VPN.
4. Specify validation methods that ensure the identity of users through the VPN.
5. Set boundaries for the IP addresses that can be used by the clients.
6. Install client software on remote users' machines.

Setting Up a VPN

To set up a VPN connection on a computer with an active Internet connection, a user should follow these steps:

1. Click the **Start** button, choose **Settings**, and then select **Control Panel**. Open **Network and Internet Connections**, and finally open **Network Connection**.
2. In the **Network Connections** window, click the **Create a new connection** link on the left-hand side of the screen.
3. The network connection wizard will lead you through the steps needed to set up a VPN connection. Select **Connect to network at my workplace**, as shown in Figure 4-4, and click the **Next** button.
4. Select **Virtual Private Network connection**, as shown in Figure 4-5, and click the **Next** button.
5. Choose an easily recognizable name for this connection and enter it into the **Company Name** text box, as shown in Figure 4-6, and click the **Next** button.
6. If the VPN should attach automatically to the ISP, choose **Automatically dial this initial connection,** and select the name of the ISP connection from the drop-down list. Otherwise, select **Do not dial the initial connection**. Click the **Next** button.

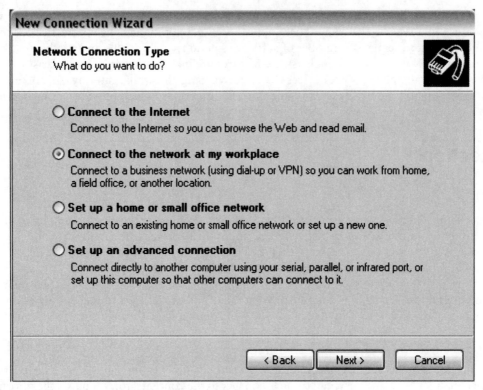

Figure 4-4   Choose **Connect to the network at my workplace.**

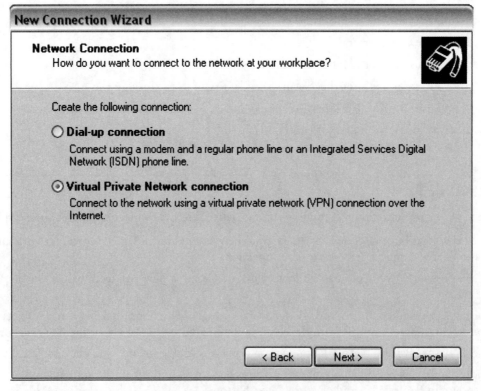

Figure 4-5   Choose **Virtual Private Network connection.**

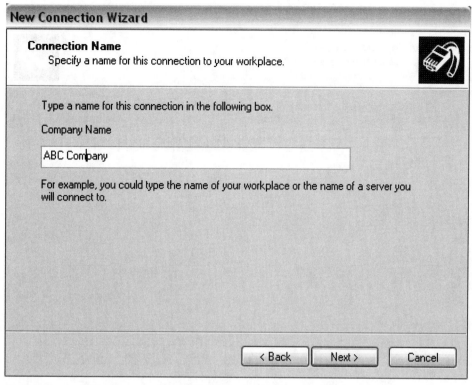

Figure 4-6   Enter an easily recognizable name as the company name.

7. In the **Host name or IP address** text box, type the hostname or IP address, as shown in Figure 4-7, and then click the **Next** button.

8. To create a shortcut icon for the VPN connection, check the **Add a shortcut to this connection to my desktop** check box shown in Figure 4-8. Otherwise, the connection can be started through **Network Connections** in Control Panel. Click the **Finish** button.

Implementing VPN Servers

Implementing DHCP Service

To implement DHCP, a user should follow these steps:

1. On the server, open the **Control Panel** and select **Add/Remove Programs**.

2. In the **Add/Remove** dialog box, click the **Add/Remove Windows Components** button.

3. Select the **Networking Services** option, and then click **Details**.

4. From the list of network services, select **Dynamic Host Configuration Protocol (DHCP)** and then click **OK**. Click **Next**. Windows will now install the DHCP service.

5. Next, the DHCP server must be created. From the **Administrative Tools** menu, select the **DHCP** option to open the DHCP console.

6. In the DHCP console, right-click on the server and select **Authorize**.

7. After authorizing the DHCP server, right-click on the server's listing within the console, and select **New Scope**. This will display the **New Scope** wizard.

8. Click **Next** to bypass the wizard's welcome screen.

9. Enter a name for the scope, and then click **Next**.

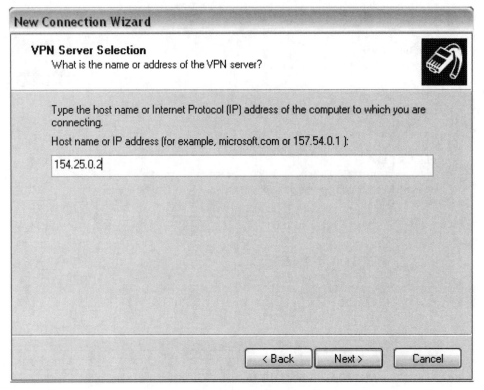

Figure 4-7   Enter the hostname or IP address.

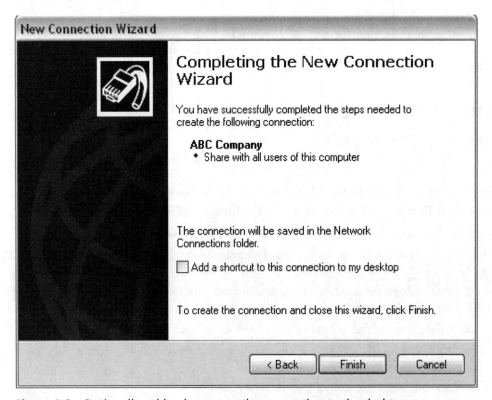

Figure 4-8   Optionally, add a shortcut to the connection to the desktop.

10. Enter a start and end address that is consistent with the existing IP addressing scheme and does not overlap any existing address. The length and subnet mask fields will be filled in automatically.

11. Click **Next** three times until the **Router (Default Gateway)** screen appears.

12. Enter the IP address of the network's default gateway, click **Add**, and then click **Next**.

13. Type the name of the domain and IP address of the DHCP server, and then click **Next**.

14. Click **Next** to skip the WINS configuration screen.

15. Verify that the **Yes, I Want to Activate the Scope Now** option is selected, click **Next**, and then click **Finish**.

Creating an Enterprise Certificate Authority

The enterprise administrator can install certificate services to create an enterprise certificate authority (CA). This provides the certificates for the purpose of digital signatures, secure e-mail using S/MIME (Secure Multipurpose Internet Mail Extensions), and authentication to a secure Web server using Secure Sockets Layer (SSL) or Transport Layer Security (TLS), and by using a smart card it will log on to the Windows Server 2003 family domain.

To install the enterprise CA in the system, the administrator should follow these steps:

1. From the Control Panel, select **Add/Remove Programs**.

2. Click **Add/Remove Windows Components** to start the **Windows Components** wizard.

3. Click **Next** after the **Welcome** window appears.

4. Check the **Certificate Services** check box from the list of components displayed.

5. Select the appropriate type from the following, and then click the **Next** button:

   - Enterprise root CA
   - Enterprise subordinate CA
   - Standalone root CA
   - Standalone subordinate CA

6. Enter a CA name and appropriate information about the organization. Click **Next**.

7. Accept the default location for the certificate database (%systemroot%\System32\CertLog). Click **Next**.

8. The service will stop and a dialog box will display if Microsoft IIS is running. Click **Next**.

9. CA files will install, along with service and system configuration data. If the system asks for the Windows disc, insert it.

10. After the wizard is done running, click **Next**. The Administrative Tools folder will now contain a shortcut for the Microsoft Management Console (MMC) Certificate Authority snap-in.

Installing IAS

To install an IAS, a user should follow these steps:

1. Click the **Start** button, open the **Control Panel**, and click **Add/Remove Windows Components**.

2. From the **Components** drop-down list, select **Networking Services**, and then click **Details**.

3. Check the **Internet Authentication Service** check box, and then click **OK**.

4. Click **Next**, and then click **Finish**.

5. Close the **Add/Remove Windows Components** dialog box.

6. To start the IAS, click **Start**, click **All Programs**, click **Administrative Tools**, and finally click **Internet Authentication Service**.

Configuring IAS

To configure an IAS, a user should follow these steps:

1. Set IAS in Active Directory to have permission to read user accounts.

2. Add a RADIUS client. In the IAS snap-in, right-click **RADIUS Clients**, and then click **New RADIUS Client Wizard** to both add and configure network access servers as RADIUS clients.

3. Delete the default remote access policies. Open the IAS snap-in, and then click **Remote Access Policies**. Select each existing policy, right-click on each policy, and then click **Delete**.

4. Create a new remote access policy. In the console tree of the IAS snap-in, right-click on **Remote Access policies,** and then click the **New Remote Access Policy Wizard** to create a policy as follows:

   • Select **Use the Wizard to setup a policy for common scenario**.

   • Type the policy name.

   • Select the access method for the policy, such as **Wireless** or **Ethernet**.

   • Under **Grant access based on the following,** click **Group,** and then click **Add**. Under **Enter the object name to select,** type the name of the security groups as defined in Active Directory. Click **OK**.

   • Select the authentication method for the users who will be placed on the VLAN. After completing the configuration of an authentication method, click **OK**.

After creating the policy, extra items must be configured for the remote access policy. The user should select **Remote Access Policies** in the IAS snap-in and then double-click the newly created policy. He or she should make changes to the policy as follows:

1. In the **Policy Properties** dialog box, select **Policy Conditions,** and click **Add**.

2. Under **Attribute Types,** click **Day-And-Time-Restriction,** and then click **Add**. In **Time of Day Restraints,** select **Permitted,** configure the days and times to allow access, and then click **OK**.

3. Click **Grant Remote Access Permission** from the **Policy Properties** dialog box.

4. Click **Edit profile,** and then click the **Advanced** tab. By default, the service type appears in attributes with the framed or specific value. For the policies with a default access method of VPN and dial-up, the framed protocol attribute appears in attributes with a value of PPP as the default protocol. To specify additional connection attributes needed for VLANs (e.g., additional connection protocols), click **Add** and then add the following:

   • **Tunnel-Medium-Type:** Select the value consistent with previous selections.

   • **Tunnel-Pvt-Group-ID:** Enter the VLAN number to which group members will be assigned.

   • **Tunnel-Type:** Select **Virtual LANs (VLAN)**.

   • **Tunnel-Tag:** Obtain this value from hardware documentation.

5. Configure IAS Connection Request policies as needed.

Creating a Remote Access Policy

1. Click **Start,** then **All Programs,** then **Administrative Tools,** and finally **Internet Authentication Service**.

2. Click **Remote Access policies**.

3. From the **Action** menu, click **New Remote Access Policy**. Create a new remote access policy.

Configuring the Remote Access Server as a Router

When using a remote access server, forward traffic inside the network. The server must be configured as a router with either static or routing protocols by following these steps:

1. Click **Start,** select **Administrative Tools,** and then click **Routing and Remote Access**.

2. Right-click on the sever name, and then click **Properties**.

3. On the **General** tab, select **Enable This Computer as a Router**.

4. Select either **Local Area Network (LAN) routing only** or **LAN and Demand-dial routing,** and then click **OK** to close the **Properties** dialog box.

Associating the VPN Server with the DHCP Server

The following are the steps to associate the VPN server with the DHCP server:

1. Navigate to the server through the Windows Explorer network console tree, select **IP Routing,** and then select the **DHCP Relay Agent**.

2. Right-click on the **DHCP Relay Agent** container and select **Properties**.

3. Enter the IP address of the DHCP server and click **Add**. Click **OK**.

Configuring Remote Clients

A special security group has to be created for any user who is going to access the network via a VPN connection. Clients should follow these steps to use the VPN connection:

1. Navigate to the **Control Panel** and open **Network and Internet Connections**.

2. Select the **Create Connection to the Network at Your Workplace** option.

3. Windows will ask if the connection will be a dial-up connection or VPN connection. Select the **VPN** option, and then click **Next**.

4. Windows will prompt for a company name. Enter a name for this VPN connection. Click **Next**.

5. Windows will prompt for a server IP address. Enter the external IP address of the VPN server. Click **Next**.

6. Click **Finish**.

Testing the Client Connection

Clients can test the client connection by following these steps:

1. In the list of available connections, double-click the VPN connection.

2. Rather than entering logon details, click the **Properties** button.

3. Select the **Networking** tab in **Properties**.

4. Set the type of VPN to **PPTP VPN**, and click **OK**.

5. Enter the username in the domain/username format.

6. Enter the password and click **Connect**.

7. If Windows asks which connection to use, select the **LAN connection** option.

8. Once connected, click **Start** and then **Run**, and enter the **\servername\ROOT** command.

VPN Policies

The VPN policy ensures that only administrators, IT staff, and authorized users can access the VPN. The VPN policy also improves the ability and flexibility to remotely access the network. Connection to a VPN is done through user accounts, while data traffic including Internet browsing uses VPN tunneling. Split tunneling is not allowed in the network sessions. *Split tunneling* is a tunneling method that allows a VPN user to access both a public network and a local area network at the same time, using the same physical network interface. The maximum time to connect to the network through the concentrator is 24 hours.

VPN Registration and Passwords

Registration is essential to secure the network connections and to identify the validity of the users of the VPN. Access is granted or rejected through security groups. When a client tries to log in to the VPN, his or her activities can be identified. Client security is an important part of the VPN's security. The user should connect to the network using a strong, secret password. The client's system should be locked when not in use even for a short time.

   Passwords must be strong. Accounts should be locked after a certain number of failed login attempts. Passwords should be encrypted for enhanced protection using either 128-bit encryption or MS-CHAP.

VPN Troubleshooting

VPN Risks

Security Risks

- Insufficient evaluation of security and legal risks from using VPNs
- Inadequate security programs

- Improper security for data before entering the VPN or after exiting the VPN
- Failure to protect information during decryption over an agreed network path
- Failure to provide privacy, reliability, nonrepudiation, and/or accessibility

Third-Party Risks

- Allowing an unsecure ISP
- Insufficient relationship management
- Improper governance and management process
- Insufficient measuring and monitoring of SLAs (service-level agreements) and metrics
- Insufficient support strategy
- Misuse of access to data on the VPN

Business Risks

- Low cost savings
- Failure to provide necessary security
- Failure to address scope and extent of user needs
- Failure or degradation of service in other areas of the company or process

Implementation Risks

- Insufficient attention to and investment in up-front design
- Unsuitable selection of VPN model
- Not enough use of appropriate third parties
- Too little attention given to security
- Unsuitable recovery processes
- Failure to plan service-level expectations and measurements
- Unsuitable integration strategy
- Unproductive change, project, or implementation management processes
- VPN client risk (same interface used for Internet and VPN traffic)

Operating Risks

- Insufficient resources to operate effectively
- Lack of dependability
- Degradation of service quality
- Poor interoperability
- Failure to provide support
- Employing of personal devices for business purposes
- Lack of security configurations, antivirus software, and personal firewalls
- Lack of confidentiality for operations or data

Implementation Review

An implementation review, conducted before the VPN is launched, can identify potential problems before they cause any damage.

Preimplementation Review

The preimplementation review should address the following:

- Planned VPN technologies, such as model, structural design, arrangement, and practice
- Planned security structural design and features
- Encryption technologies
- Planned redundancy and support facilities
- Administrative approvals
- Intended project administration structures and scrutiny mechanisms
- Selection process of the service provider
- Planned contracts, SLAs, and metrics
- Legal requirements

To address these aspects, the auditor should:

- Study the VPN needs, including both business and technical requirements.
- Study the business case (costs and benefits) and approvals.
- Review the VPN design document outlining the technology aspects.
- Review whether the proposed solution would be best for PPTP, L2TP, or IPSec.
- Review the projected security architecture and encryption technology.
- Evaluate the technical and commercial alternate proposals and the required service provider.
- Learn the proposed project management structure.
- Study the proposed contracts, SLAs, and metrics.
- Study the statutory needs to be fulfilled.
- Estimate the redundancy and backups proposed.
- Review the strategy proposed to integrate the VPN with the applications.
- Use external experts wherever necessary to evaluate the appropriateness of the technology and security aspects.
- Learn the designed training plans.
- Learn any associated audit/review reports.
- Examine the security risks, third-party risks, business risks, implementation risks, and operating risks mentioned previously.
- Estimate how COBIT (Control Objectives for Information and Related Technology) and CONCT (Control Objectives for Net Centric Technology) aspects are being satisfied.

Implementation Review

During the review of the implementation, the auditor needs to ensure the following:

- Implementation is done with respect to the agreed plans, time constraints, and specified costs.
- Model, architecture, setup type, and use of VPN technology are implemented as defined.
- Encryption techniques and security policies are applied as specified.
- Duplication and backup facilities are used as designed.
- Requirement specifications are met in assigning contracts and SLAs.
- All important requirements are managed.
- Project development reports are maintained.
- Differences between plan and implementation are noted.

- The solution is compatible with standard protocols such as PPTP, L2TP, and IPSec.
- The contracts and SLAs that have been agreed upon are understood by all parties.
- The VPN is compatible with existing applications.
- All processes related to bandwidth, access control, and encryption are tested.
- Billing systems are verified.
- Legacy connections that do not use VPN are removed.
- Auditing and risk management are implemented.
- Risks in different levels such as business, security, implementation, and operation are addressed.
- COBIT and CONCT criteria are satisfied.

Review results should be noted and acted upon to resolve the related risks.

Postimplementation Review

After the implementation of the VPN, a postimplementation review is conducted to ensure:

- Anticipated advantages outweigh the expenditures.
- The objective of VPN technology is achieved and its usage conforms to predefined security policies.
- Data classification must be done as specified.
- Third parties who use the VPN sign the proper forms that specify the permissions and agree to the security policies.
- The security features for the remote clients are implemented as defined.
- Digital certificates are implemented.
- There is regular supervision of SLAs, metrics, and QoS.
- Incoming and outgoing data are verified.
- Security tools are used to ensure protection from viruses and intrusions.

The auditor needs to ensure the following to address the above requirements:

- Report of project completion.
- Developed VPN technologies match the actual design.
- Solutions are compatible with PPTP, L2TP, and IPSec.
- Bills are reviewed.
- Procedures are secure.
- Proper security tools are employed.

Reporting

Reports should contain these concepts:

- The scope, aim, and methods followed
- Complete assessment of solutions with flaws and strengths
- Suggestions to mitigate any flaws

VPN Product Testing

VPN product testing verifies that the VPN does the following securely:

- Allows a point-to-point secure connection between two networks
- Allows a secured point-to-point connection between roaming clients and the Internet
- Provides authentication and access control mechanisms to restrict resource access
- Provides packet filtering or proxy services within the tunnel to control the traffic to exact protocols or source/destination points

- Provides a sensible level of encryption and data integrity for the data within the VPN tunnel
- Provides a protected key-exchange method for all VPN devices

There are other tests that can be conducted, including penetration tests and encryption tests, as well as benchmark testing to improve performance.

Common VPN Flaws

VPN Fingerprinting

Several VPN servers can be fingerprinted by UDP back-off fingerprinting or vendor ID fingerprinting. This can give useful information to a potential attacker. Some systems will expose the general type of device (such as Cisco PIX or Nortel Contivity), while other systems will display the software version details.

The Ike-scan tool, shown in Figure 4-9, can be used to fingerprint the server vendor and version number of IPSec VPNs. This tool compares the specific variables in IPSec packets being exchanged with the values in its signature database.

The information obtained during the fingerprinting process provides a good deal of information regarding the VPN's vulnerabilities. It enables a knowledgeable attacker to attempt attacks with known vulnerabilities for the specific type of VPN, as well as guess its username and password.

Ike-scan uses its own retransmission strategy to deal with lost packets in order to fingerprint the VPN server. The IKE packet that is sent to probe the VPN is designed so that it does not reply to the VPN server's responses. This makes the server believe that the packets are lost, and the server then tries to resend the lost packets depending on its back-off strategy. Information such as the time difference between the corresponding packets received can be used to determine the back-off strategy, which in turn helps to fingerprint the server.

The —showbackoff option of Ike-scan records the response time of all packets and delays for 60 seconds after the last packet is received. This delay ensures that all the packets are received prior to displaying times and performing pattern matching. Because of this, the back-off fingerprinting process takes between one and two minutes.

The —ikeprobe option, shown in Figure 4-10, identifies vulnerabilities in the preshared key (PSK) implementation of the VPN server. By trying various combinations of ciphers, hashes, and Diffie-Helman groups, —ikeprobe forces the VPN server into aggressive mode.

IKECrack is another tool, designed to use brute force and dictionary attacks to crack the passwords for PSK authentication in VPNs.

Insecure Storage of Authentication Credentials by VPN Clients

VPN usage introduces security risks, particularly if the credentials are not protected. The following are some common client issues:

- *Storing the unencrypted username in a file or the registry*: In this case, anyone with access to the client computer can obtain the username. If the VPN is using IKE aggressive mode, an attacker who has the username can perform an offline attack against the password.

- *Storing the password in a scrambled form*: When a password is stored in scrambled form, there is no key to decrypt it. But if the decryption algorithm is known, it is easy to crack the password.

```
G:\ike-VPN-test>ike-scan 10.0.0.1

Starting ike-scan 1.6 with 1 hosts (http://www.nta-monitor.com/ike-scan/)

10.0.0.1 Main Mode Handshake returned SA=(Enc=3DES Hash=SHA1 Auth=PSK
Group=1:modp768 LifeT

ype=Seconds LifeDuration(4)=0x00007080)


Ending ike-scan 1.6: 1 hosts scanned in 0.979 seconds (1.02 hosts/sec).

1 returned handshake; 0 returned notify
```

Figure 4-9   Ike-scan fingerprints the server vendor and version number of IPSec VPNs.

```
IKEProbe 0.1beta   (c) 2003 Michael Thumann (www.ernw.de)

Portions Copyright (c) 2003 Cipherica Labs (www.cipherica.com)

Read license-cipherica.txt for LibIKE License Information

IKE Aggressive Mode PSK Vulnerability Scanner (Bugtraq ID 7423)


Supported Attributes
Ciphers             : DES, 3DES, AES-128, CAST
Hashes              : MD5, SHA1
Diffie Hellman Groups: DH Groups 1,2 and 5


IKE Proposal for Peer: 10.0.0.2
Aggressive Mode activated ...


[Output truncated for brevity]
Cipher AES
Hash MD5
Diffie Hellman Group 2


841.890 3: ph1_initiated(00443ee0, 007d23c8)
841.950 3: << ph1 (00443ee0, 276)
843.963 3: << ph1 (00443ee0, 276)
846.967 3: << ph1 (00443ee0, 276)
849.961 3: ph1_disposed(00443ee0)


   1.   Attribute Settings:
Cipher AES
Hash MD5
Diffie Hellman Group 5


849.961 3: ph1_initiated(00443ee0, 007d5010)
849.141 3: << ph1 (00443ee0, 340)
851.644 3: << ph1 (00443ee0, 340)
854.648 3: << ph1 (00443ee0, 340)
857.652 3: ph1_disposed(00443ee0)
```

Figure 4-10   The —ikeprobe option identifies vulnerabilities and forces the VPN server into aggressive mode.

- *Storing the plaintext password in memory*: If passwords are stored in plaintext in memory, they can be retrieved by dumping the physical memory using tools such as PMDump. Figure 4-11 shows an example of output from PMDump.

- *Weak registry or file permissions for stored credentials*: It is a bad idea to store credentials at all, but it is much worse if they are placed in an easily accessible file or registry entry, as shown in Figure 4-12.

Username Enumeration Vulnerabilities

Remote access VPNs use IKE aggressive mode with preshared key (PSK) authentication as the default authentication technique. Username/password authentication requires that the response to an incorrect login does not give any information that would assist an attacker, such as which credential was incorrect.

Figure 4-13 shows an aggressive mode PSK authentication packet exchange. In this process, the client transfers an IKE packet to the VPN server, and the VPN server responds with another IKE packet. Both packets include many ISAKMP payloads, including the identity payload sent by the client, that includes the username and the hash payload given by the server. This is an HMAC hash of different things, including the password. In an actual authentication process, the client responds with a third packet containing an HMAC hash of several things, including the password.

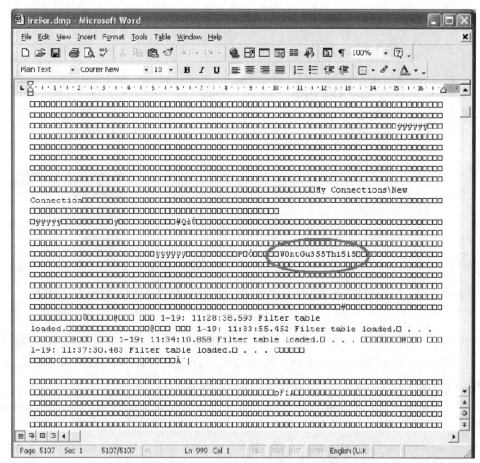

Source: http://www.nta-monitor.com/posts/2005/01/VPN-Flaws-Whitepaper.pdf. Accessed 2005.

Figure 4-11 If passwords are stored in memory in plaintext form, the memory can be dumped to retrieve them.

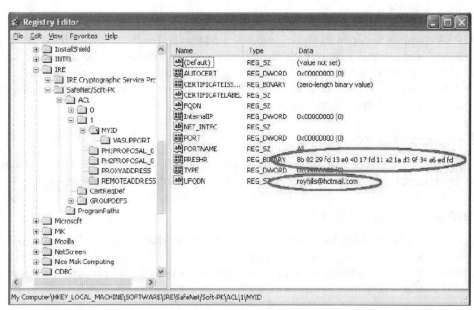

Source: http://www.nta-monitor.com/posts/2005/01/VPN-Flaws-Whitepaper.pdf. Accessed 2005.

Figure 4-12 Credentials should never be stored in easily accessible files or the registry.

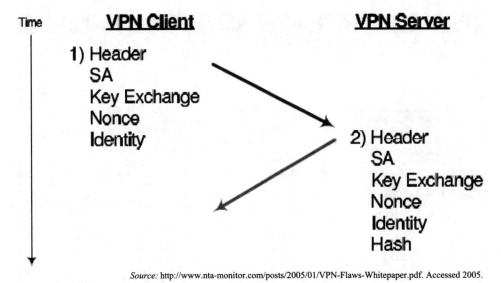

Source: http://www.nta-monitor.com/posts/2005/01/VPN-Flaws-Whitepaper.pdf. Accessed 2005.

Figure 4-13 This shows an aggressive mode PSK authentication packet exchange.

There are three faults in the way the VPN servers respond to the first packet from the client:

1. Some VPN servers do not respond to all usernames. They only respond if the client has a valid username.

2. Some VPN servers will respond with a notification message.

3. Some VPN servers reply to both correct and incorrect usernames, but for invalid usernames, a hash payload is calculated using a null password, and it is easy for the client to determine it.

In all three situations, the response for an invalid username is different from that for a valid username, which permits the client to determine if a username is valid or not. After getting a correct username with IKE aggressive mode, it is simple to get a hash from the VPN server and to use this hash to brute-force-crack the password.

The correct procedure for a VPN server to respond for an incorrect username is to use a random password for the hash payload. It is easy to implement and does not permit the user to check whether the username is correct or not.

Man-In-The-Middle Attacks

An ISAKMP SA (Internet Security Association and Key Management Protocol Security Association) is set up on the VPN server if it is using IKE aggressive mode and is able to identify a valid username and password. Even if the VPN server implements a second level of authentication, this frequently depends on the security level of the ISAKMP SA. Even the second level of authentication will not provide complete security because it is still vulnerable to a man-in-the-middle attack.

Lack of Account Lockout

Generally, operating systems permit accounts to be locked out after a number of incorrect login attempts. Still, many VPN implementations do not support this and permit unlimited login attempts.

Poor Default Configurations

Most VPN server configurations are geared for usability rather than security. Typically, IKE aggressive mode with a preshared key is a default authentication method, even when stronger authentication techniques are available. Some servers are configured with weak ciphers by default, which are much easier for an attacker to crack.

Poor Guidance and Documentation

Many VPN implementations do not provide adequate documentation to explain different configurations. When setting up a VPN, an administrator should always consult an expert whenever anything is unclear.

Chapter Summary

■ Virtual private networks, or VPNs, allow secure connectivity over unsecure networks, including the Internet.

■ There are several types of VPNs, including internal LAN VPNs, remote access VPNs, and extranet VPNs.

■ VPNs use a mechanism called tunneling, which is a virtual connection between the source and destination that involves encapsulating data packets using a security protocol in order to make them impossible to read if intercepted.

■ There are two types of VPN tunneling: voluntary tunneling and compulsory tunneling.

■ Popular VPN tunneling protocols include the following: Point-to-Point Tunneling Protocol (PPTP), Layer Two Tunneling Protocol (L2TP), and Internet Protocol Security (IPSec).

■ VPN provides the following: client privacy, data reliability, and information authenticity.

■ The VPN policy ensures that only administrators, IT staff, and authorized users can access the VPN.

Review Questions

1. What is a VPN?

_____

_____

_____

_____

2. What are the types of VPNs?

_____

_____

_____

_____

3. What is voluntary tunneling?

_____

_____

_____

_____

4. What is compulsory tunneling?

_____

_____

_____

_____

5. What are the VPN tunneling protocols?

_____

_____

_____

_____

6. How is a VPN set up?

_____

_____

_____

7. How are DHCP services implemented?

_____

_____

_____

_____

8. How are remote clients configured?

_____

_____

_____

_____

9. What are VPN policies?

_____

_____

_____

_____

10. What are some risks associated with VPNs?

_____

_____

_____

_____

11. What is an implementation review?

_____

_____

_____

_____

12. What are some common VPN flaws?

_____

_____

_____

_____

Hands-On Projects

1. Read an introduction to VPN.

   ■ Navigate to Chapter 4 of the Student Resource Center.

   ■ Open Introduction to VPN.pdf and read the content.

2. Read how to connect to a VPN.

   ■ Navigate to Chapter 4 of the Student Resource Center.

   ■ Open Connect to Your Virtual Private Network.pdf and read the content.

3. Read how to enable a secure VPN.

   ■ Navigate to Chapter 4 of the Student Resource Center.

   ■ Open Enabling Secure vpn.pdf and read the content.

4. Read about the benefits of VPNs.

   ■ Navigate to Chapter 4 of the Student Resource Center.

   ■ Open Benefits Virtual Private Networks.pdf and read the content.

5. Read about VPN security flaws.

   ■ Navigate to Chapter 4 of the Student Resource Center.

   ■ Open VPN-Flaws-Whitepaper.pdf and read the content.

Chapter 5

Creating Fault Tolerance

Objectives

After completing this chapter, you should be able to:

- Plan for fault tolerance
- Identify reasons for system failure
- Understand preventive measures
- Understand RAID levels
- Conduct deployment testing

Key Terms

Disk striping   the process of spreading a single logical volume across multiple disks to increase performance

Disk striping with parity   a type of disk striping that produces an additional stripe that contains the parity information and allows for the restoration of any lost information from a failed disk in the disk set and thus is fault tolerant; this technique requires a minimum of three hard disks in the disk set

Failover system   a system that automatically takes over operations upon the failure of any of the primary critical system functions

File synchronization   the process of updating files stored at different locations with the newest changes to those files

Mirrors   accurate copies of the data on one disk transferred to another disk

Parity bit   a bit that indicates that an error has occurred in transmission and the received data are corrupted

Tape autochanger   a device that automatically rotates backup tapes

Introduction to Creating Fault Tolerance

Computer systems are not perfect. Nearly every system acts unpredictably from time to time, ranging from small glitches to catastrophic failures. In order to deal with these problems, it is important to create an adequate level of fault tolerance. Fault tolerance is the capability of a system to recover from any unpredicted hardware, software, or power failures. This chapter teaches you how to make sure your systems are fault tolerant, in order to better ensure the availability and reliability of resources.

Planning for Fault Tolerance

To implement fault tolerance, an administrator should follow these basic steps:

1. Recognize the components in the network that are likely to cause failure.

2. Prioritize the threats in order of most to least likely to occur.

3. Execute solutions to these threats.

Some fault-tolerance measures discussed in this chapter include archiving files using RAID, clustering, maintaining backups of files, and storing important documents as read-only.

Careful planning is necessary to guarantee that the fault-tolerant systems execute as expected. This can be done using the Cooperative Intelligent Real-Time Control Architecture (CIRCA) model, as follows:

1. First, plan for the allocation of resources in case a resource fails. Identify which resources have the most demand.

2. Create a plan to deal with resource faults.

3. Use resource allocation algorithms to map the required resources with available resources at regular intervals. Each processor has a set of schedulable resources.

4. Depending on the platform used, any processor that schedules plans for resource allocation should either accept the failure due to broadcast or accept the new schedules and work regardless of transmission delay.

Two very important resources are the processors and transmission lines. When planning interfaces to allocate resources, consider if the current implemented plans for fault-tolerant systems can be scheduled so as to not unreasonably interfere with the normal use and operation of those resources. If not, reschedule the plans for resource allocation.

Aspects of Fault Tolerance

Some key aspects of fault tolerance are:

- Improves system reliability
- Saves bandwidth for data transfer by using efficient scheduling
- Improves customer service
- Improves content management
- Improves security with authentication and firewalls
- Minimizes system administration requirements
- Protects from network failures, server failures, and natural disasters

Reasons for System Failure

Systems can fail for any number of reasons, including crime, user error, the environment, and routine events.

Crime

Hacking

A hacker that gains access to a system can cause a huge amount of damage. Small attacks can create problems like denials of service and network failure, while larger attacks can corrupt, destroy, or steal data. Hackers can change system settings, but they generally cannot cause hardware damage.

To avoid hacking issues, the administrator should do the following:

- Secure the network against unauthorized access.
- Give user accounts the least necessary privileges.
- Regularly back up data.

Virus or Worm Outbreak

Vulnerabilities in operating systems allow viruses and worms to infect systems and spread at an alarming rate. These malicious programs can destroy or corrupt data on an infected system, as well as steal large amounts of bandwidth. To avoid issues with worms and viruses, the administrator should apply operating system and software updates as soon as they become available.

Theft of Offline Data

Disgruntled employees or attackers can steal the physical disks that store important data. To avoid offline data theft, administrators should do the following:

- Provide physical security to systems.
- Back up files daily.

Sabotage

Sometimes, unsatisfied employees will sabotage a network from the inside, causing heavy damage with legitimate credentials. This can also happen due to corporate espionage from the outside.

To avoid sabotage, the administrator should do the following:

- Ensure adequate physical security and restrict access to valuable files as much as possible.
- Monitor and track user actions.

Terrorism

Government agencies have recently increased their network security against terrorist attacks, but plans should still be made in order to deal with them should they occur. In order to provide continuity of operations after a terrorist attack, administrators should maintain offsite backups of all critical data.

User Error

The majority of computer downtime in business is due to human errors, including the following:

- Overwriting or deleting files
- Changing operating system configurations
- Applying patches before testing
- Incompletely setting up software
- Using newer software with undiscovered vulnerabilities

To prevent and recover from user errors, the administrator should do the following:

- Give user accounts the least necessary privileges to prevent them from deleting important files.
- Back up files daily.

Environment

Fire

If fires are not caught early, they can be very difficult to control. A large fire can cause a huge amount of damage to everything, including computer systems.

Countermeasures to fire include the following:

- Place fire and smoke detectors.
- Maintain offsite backups.

Water

While a full flood can obviously cause damage to all physical assets, even a small amount of water can destroy a computer system. This water could enter the area through a leaky roof, a malfunctioning air conditioning system, or even condensation from ambient moisture.

To avoid water damage, the administrator should do the following:

- Make sure server rooms are above ground level.
- Maintain offsite backups, and store local backups above ground level.

Earthquake

It is important to know if the local area is prone to earthquakes. If there is any chance of earthquakes, the administrator should make sure systems are physically secured and maintain offsite backups.

Routine Events

Hardware Failures

Many things can cause hardware failure. For instance, if hardware is left unused for a long period of time, it can fail. On the other hand, if hardware is used too often, it can wear out. Proper management is required to prevent device failure.

Mean time between failures (MTBF) is the amount of time electrical equipment can be expected to perform adequately. The general MTBF for hard disks is five years. There are two common reasons for hard disk failure:

1. Constant hard disk access, usually in servers
2. Heat consuming the lubricant in the disk's spindle

Copies of data should be maintained in a second, backup hard disk of the same system or other removable device.

To avoid problems with hardware failure, the administrator should do the following:

- Implement RAID 1 or RAID 5.
- Back up data daily.
- Handle hardware devices with care.

Software Failures

Undetected bugs and vulnerabilities can cause total software failure. If two pieces of software are incompatible with one another, they may both fail to execute.

To avoid problems with software failure, the administrator should do the following:

- Test software before implementing it.
- Check for documented incompatibilities between different software applications and operating systems.

Power Failures

Power failures occur when power consumption increases beyond the transmission capacity. Power transmitters are usually built to be fault tolerant, but it is still important to use uninterruptible power supplies (UPSs) and power generators in case something does go wrong.

Network Circuit Failures

Circuit failures make the network unavailable to its users. The administrator should employ robust circuits and install redundant routers to provide easy and failover system access to the network. A *failover system* is a system that automatically takes over operations upon the failure of any of the primary critical system functions.

Preventive Measures

There are a few things that can prevent faults from occurring in the first place, including the following:

- Data backup
- UPSs and power generators

- Perimeter security
- Physical security
- Offsite storage

Backup

Backups are a general form of fault tolerance and are very important in recovering from any type of failure. Backups are snapshots of all data on a machine at a particular time and are kept on external devices like tapes.

Backup Method

Tapes used for backup are attached to the server. The organization's night staff is responsible for changing tapes and initiating the copy process. Tapes are labeled according to the time and date the backups were carried out.

Once a tape is used, it should ideally not be reused, so it can be a permanent record of the state of the network on that date. On the other hand, smaller organizations may rotate a certain number of tapes, overwriting the oldest backup every night.

Archive Marking

Archive marking is a method used by all operating systems to show which files have been altered since the last backup. This is done through a single bit flag attached to every file as an attribute. The archive bit is placed every time a file is written and can only be zeroed by archive software. Therefore, every file containing this bit has been modified and is different from the most recent backup. Most backup software allows the user to back up only those files that have been modified since the last backup. This can save both time and storage space.

Backup Options

Most backup software contains the following backup options:

- *Full backup*: Full backup archives every file on the system and erases all archive bits.
- *Copy backup*: Copy backup archives every file on the computer without changing the archive bit flags. Copy operations take less time and can archive read-only files, because there is no need to open any files to zero out bit flags.
- *Incremental backup*: Incremental backup archives each file with its archive bit set and resets the bit.
- *Differential backup*: Differential backup archives every file that has its archive bit set, but it does not reset the bit, so the next backup will still include recently modified data as new data.
- *Periodic backup*: Periodic backup archives all files that have been modified since a specified date.
- *Image backup*: In an image backup, a complete copy of the disk is written to tape, including all information necessary to reconstruct the drive's partitions. This backs up every single bit of the disk, including any open files.

Tape Backup Features

Tape devices vary from simple single cartridge units to complicated, automated tape changers. *Tape autochangers* are devices that automatically rotate backup tapes. When one tape is filled to maximum, the next tape in the changer is rotated in and the archive operation continues. This makes it possible to archive large amounts of data. This does, however, add time to the backup operation, and these devices may fail.

Redundant Array of Independent Tapes (RAIT), also called Tape RAID, is an alteration of RAID (Redundant Array of Independent Disks) technology. RAIT uses several tape devices in parallel, depending on the volume of the data to be backed up. RAIT is usually inexpensive and faster than tape autochangers. They are faster, because all tapes are used simultaneously, so it takes no more time than making a single backup tape.

Problems with Tape Backup   Unfortunately, tape backup is very unreliable. As many as two-thirds of efforts to completely rebuild a system from a tape backup will be unsuccessful. This failure is often due to human error. Employees have to change the tape every day, and they may forget to do so. If the backup software determines that the tape has not been changed, it will either not run a backup at all, or it will run a new backup, replacing the old one.

Practical Backup Tips

- Backup is very important, and administrators should set aside an adequate part of the budget to cover the expenses that daily backups incur.

- Use media large enough to perform a whole backup onto a single tape. If this is not possible, use RAIT software.

- Maintain automated backup software to minimize dependence on humans.

- Use image backup software rather than file-based backup software. This makes recovery far easier.

- Turn off disk-based catalogs. They take up far more space than necessary, and they are not available when computers crash. Use media-based catalogs.

- Use software with an open-file backup feature so that important, open files can be backed up.

- Use the Windows *force system logoff* user policy to close down user connections and force all files to close just prior to the backup.

- Mark media each time it is written. Throw away reusable media after their tenth backup.

- Do a full system backup at least once a week, and store the backup for whatever period of time is required by your security policy.

- Test the backups by implementing full system restores to test servers at least once per quarter.

- Do not spend time and resources backing up workstations. Inform users that important files should be stored on network file servers.

- Workstations should contain operating system and application files only, all of which can be easily recovered by reinstalling software from CD-ROMs.

- Use enterprise-based backup software that can transmit backup data over the network to a central backup server. Make sure this backup occurs overnight so it does not degrade network performance.

UPSs and Power Generators

Uninterruptible power supplies (UPSs) are battery systems that provide continued power during a power failure. This gives users a few extra minutes to save their work and properly shut down their workstations. UPSs are not designed to run through long power outages, so if power is not restored within a few minutes, servers must be shut down as well.

UPSs are common and can be acquired through any computer retail channel. Setup simply involves plugging the UPS into the power source and then plugging the computer into the UPS. Some models also include serial or USB connections that can tell a computer to shut down. They also normalize poorly regulated power, extending the life of the computer's internal power supply and reducing the likelihood of the power supply causing a fire.

While it can be helpful to use UPSs on workstations, it is only really necessary for servers that store critical data. Administrators should remember to put UPSs on hubs and routers if servers will need to communicate with one another during a power failure event. If the entire system must be operational during a power failure, emergency power generators are needed, which are extremely expensive. These generators are started within a few minutes after the main power failure, while computers are still running on their UPS systems. As soon as the power generators are delivering power, the UPS systems return to their normal condition. When main power is reestablished, the generators shut down again.

Once UPSs and power generators are in position, it is important to test the conditions of a power failure before one actually occurs. After working hours, administrators should turn off the main power and make sure that all the servers close down correctly. Servers can be configured to restart manually once power is restored or to wait until they are manually restarted.

Perimeter Security

Firewalls should have the following characteristics to provide adequate security:

- *Information protection*: Firewalls should not disclose anything about the interior of the network, or even disclose their presence. When hackers scan for networks using ping scanners, they depend upon the victim to respond. Firewalls should not respond to these scans. This means that technologies such as

Simple Network Management Protocol (SNMP) should not be used to manage firewalls, and administrators should only be able to reach the firewall from the private interface.

- *Connection control*: Firewalls can control all data that passes between the company's network and the Internet. This is the most significant measure taken to control security on the network. Wireless network access points, modems, and any other method of transmitting data must be assessed in terms of network security.

- *Demilitarized zone*: If two different levels of security for different purposes are needed, a separate firewall must be installed behind the machines that require expanded Internet access so that if they are compromised, the rest of the network is safe. This configuration is called a demilitarized zone (DMZ). This should be used to divide public servers such as e-mail and Web servers from the internal network while providing firewall protection.

- *Universal policy*: A specific type of traffic must be controlled in the same way at all firewalls. If a protocol is allowed to pass one firewall, it does not matter if every other firewall blocks it. Enterprise-level firewalls, such as Check Point FireWall-1, allow users to set a single policy and then apply it to all firewalls.

- *Deny by default*: All traffic except that which the firewall knows it must accept should be rejected, including both incoming and outgoing data. The effect of becoming infected with a virus or worm is greatly reduced if the malicious software cannot open an outgoing connection.

Physical Security

Good physical security on the premises is very important. Software security measures will do very little good if the premises can be physically breached. Physical security measures include locks on entrances, security guards, and video surveillance.

Centralization is important in all aspects of security. It is much easier to keep server and computer resources physically secure if they are located in the same room or group of rooms on each floor or in each building. Allocating servers throughout the organization is a great way to increase overall bandwidth, but these servers must be thoroughly secured physically.

There are several types of locks that can be used, including key locks, combination locks, and biometric locks. Keys can be stolen, and combinations can be accidentally revealed to third parties, but biometric sensors such as handprint scanners or retinal scanners cannot be fooled.

A secure space has secure lock mechanisms on each door, locks that cannot simply be detached from the door, doors that cannot be detached from the outside space, and no available access other than those doors. It does not have glass windows, a drop ceiling joined to other rooms, flimsy walls, or ventilation ducts large enough to crawl through.

Good alarm systems can mechanically call the police, integrate with fire alarms, and page responsible employees when alarms go off. Security guards are a very effective deterrent to direct intrusion attempts, but they are, of course, expensive.

Offsite Storage

Offsite storage is the process of sending data to another location so that if anything catastrophic occurs at the original system, the backups or archives are not damaged. There are two ways to handle offsite storage:

1. Physically moving backup media to another location on a regular basis

2. Passing data to another facility using a network, such as the Internet

Using the Internet is far more dependable, because it can be automated, removing human error. It is important to be sure that there is enough bandwidth to finish the operation before the next operation queues up, so testing is very important. File management software can be configured so that only changed data are sent, lessening the bandwidth load.

Redundant Array of Independent Disks (RAID)

Redundant Array of Independent Disks, or RAID, describes multiple disks combined into a single logical volume. This means that if a disk fails, another disk contains the same data, so nothing is lost. Except for RAID level 0, at least one hard disk can fail and the system will remain usable. The system does not even need to shut down for the failed drive to be substituted with a new one. There are six RAID levels: 0–5.

RAID Level 0

This is not considered fault tolerance, because all data is still only stored once. One disk's malfunction can cause the entire volume to fail. Because of this, RAID 0 is not suitable for servers. This is a form of *disk striping*, when a single logical volume is spread across multiple disks to increase performance.

Figure 5-1 shows a RAID 0 configuration.

RAID Level 1

RAID 1 implements *mirrors*, which are accurate copies of the data on one disk transferred to another disk. This supports fault tolerance because if a single disk fails, its data can be retrieved from the mirror copy made on the other disk. This requires two disks of the exact same type and model. If models are different, it may cause speed synchronization issues affecting disk performance.

RAID 1 implementations require a RAID 1 controller. In some software and operating systems, mirroring is executed using the disk manager. Hardware and software mirroring are very trustworthy and can be executed on any server.

Figure 5-2 shows a RAID 1 configuration.

RAID Level 2

RAID 2 uses *disk striping with parity*, a type of disk striping that produces an additional stripe that contains the parity information and allows for the restoration of any lost information from a failed disk in the disk set and thus is fault tolerant. This technique requires a minimum of three hard disks in the disk set. The *parity bit* is a bit that indicates that an error has occurred in transmission and the received data are corrupted. RAID 2 is highly complex and rarely used, but is sometimes used for commercial purposes. RAID 2 also uses byte-level striping with a form of error-correcting code (ECC) known as *Hamming code*. The number of disks required for configuration of RAID 2 may vary, but it typically uses 14 disk drives: 10 data disks and 4 Error Correcting Code (ECC) disks.

Figure 5-3 shows a RAID 2 configuration.

RAID Level 3

This is similar to RAID 0, but one drive in the array is used for storing error correction data, making a CRC (cyclic redundancy check) checksum on data written to other disks. RAID 3 provides redundancy by writing

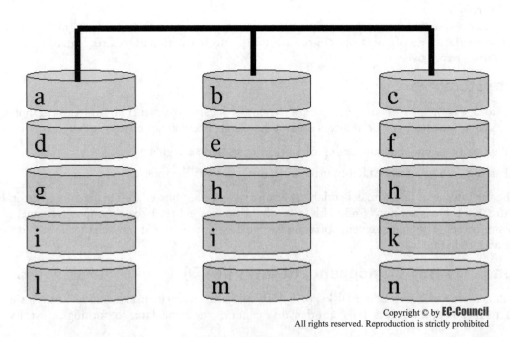

Figure 5-1   RAID 0 does not include any fault tolerance.

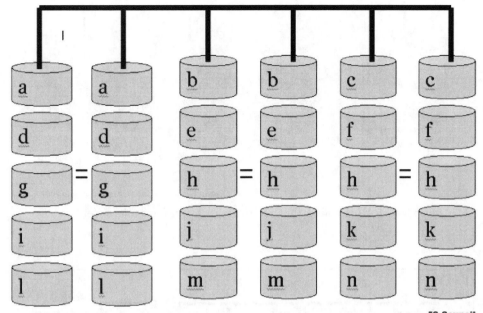

Figure 5-2   RAID 1 includes mirrors of all data on separate disks.

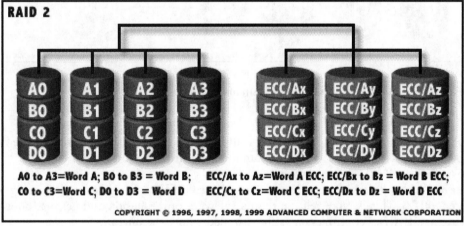

Figure 5-3   RAID 2 is rarely used due to its high complexity.

all data to three or more disks. This is ideal for systems requiring large file transfers, including videos, images, streaming, and publishing.

RAID 3 uses the XOR algorithm for parity generation. It is shown in Figure 5-4.

RAID Level 4

RAID 4 is similar to RAID 3, with the major difference being that RAID 4 uses block-level striping. This means that the stripe size can be changed to meet application requirements.

RAID 4 needs at least three disks. It also delivers good performance and fault tolerance like RAID 3, but performs better for smaller file access like database transaction processing instead of large sequential files.

Figure 5-5 shows a RAID 4 configuration.

RAID Level 5

RAID 5 creates disk sets or disk packs of multiple drives in a single logical volume. A single disk holds parity information with a mathematical sum of the information contained in the other stripes spread across all disks. This disk is equal to the size of one drive in the set, and is used to store a copy of the data on any one disk. In

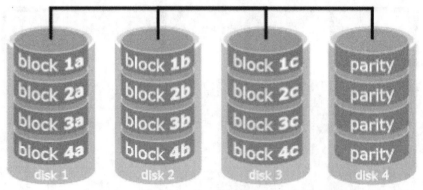

Figure 5-4   RAID 3 delivers both performance and fault tolerance.

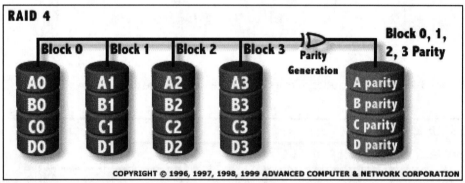

Figure 5-5   RAID 4 is more useful for smaller file access than is RAID 3.

the event of a disk failure, data can be automatically retrieved from the information stored on the other disks and the parity stripe. This method requires a minimum of three hard disks.

Figure 5-6 shows a RAID 5 configuration.

At higher levels, fault tolerance requires hardware-based RAID 5. For this, low-level programming is put into the computer's BIOS. This is more reliable than a software-only solution and permits booting directly from a RAID 5 partition. RAID 5 controllers must be installed before the operating system.

RAID 0+1: Striping with Mirroring

RAID 0+1, also known as RAID 10, combines RAID 0 striping with RAID 1 mirroring. It makes two RAID 0 stripe sets and mirrors across them. This method can tolerate the failure of half of the disks. For example, if there is a stripe set of three 40-GB disks to create a 120-GB volume, RAID 10 can mirror that stripe set to an identical set of three 40-GB disks. The total storage remains 120 GB.

With the same six disks, RAID 5 only allows 100 GB of storage with the same level of fault tolerance. Hardware RAID 5 controllers are costly because a microprocessor must be used to assess the parity information. RAID 10 controllers, on the other hand, are inexpensive, because no additional hardware is needed.

Clustered Servers

Clustering involves running a single application on multiple machines simultaneously. In addition to providing fault tolerance, this is useful for very demanding applications, like enterprise databases, commercial Web sites, and serious scientific applications.

Failover Clustering

Failover clustering, also called server replication, is the process of retaining an auxiliary server in operation that can take over without human intervention in the event of the failure of the main server. In general, these

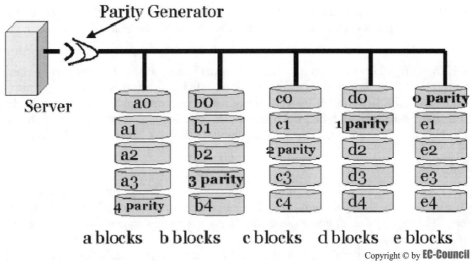

Figure 5-6 RAID 5 presents disk sets as a single logical volume.

clusters use disk systems that can be changed from one machine to another without human intervention, or they automatically apply changes to the disk from the main server to the secondary server. Failover clustering does not permit multiple servers to handle identical services at the same time. Responsibility is simply shifted to another member of the cluster if a system crash occurs.

Stateless Protocol

Stateless protocols do not keep any information about the client session on the server side. This means that they can be effortlessly clustered across multiple machines without worrying about data, because it does not matter to which server the client connects from one case to the next.

Information accumulated in RAM on the servers is not retained, so even though the server may change, open network sessions will be lost unless they are using stateless protocols like HTTP. If the primary server fails, sessions can be reestablished on new servers without any difficulty or human intervention. This is not useful for application services such as SQL server and messaging servers, because those applications are responsible for moving data between the members of the cluster.

Stateless clustering was designed for Web services for large sites, and it works very well for those services. The quantity of user information stored on a Web site is usually much less than the amount of data sent to each user. Because some Web sites need to handle millions of concurrent sessions, this method allows designers to put the client-handling load on Web servers and keep the database load on back-end database servers.

Load Balancing

Load balancing is a clustering method in which single client sessions are connected to any one of a number of similarly configured servers, so that the complete load of client sessions is stretched regularly among these servers. This permits multiple machines to act in response to the same IP address and stabilizes the client load. This makes all the servers act as one server that can handle a huge number of concurrent connections. Both Windows and UNIX maintain this type of clustering.

Load balancing is not meant for file services, databases, or e-mail because there is no standard way to duplicate data stored on one server to all the rest of the servers. If the user stores a file on one server in the cluster, it may not be there when that user accesses a different server in the cluster. This problem can be solved by configuring all clustered machines to send their accumulated data to a single back-end storage or database server.

Simple Server Redundancy

Simple server redundancy is the method of replicating or swapping out an entire server. It is required at sites where downtime costs are extremely high. Simple server redundancy can be configured as follows:

- Assign more than one IP address to a single domain name rather than to a single server. The other servers in the domain continuously ping the primary server address and if the primary server does not respond, each in turn will take over. This way, an array of Web servers with identical IP addresses can be used. As each server is identical, the client would get the same data from the server to which he or she has been attached.

- Firewalls can be organized to load-balance a single IP address across a group of identical machines.
- Cross-copying files between two or more servers maintains a complete copy of all data on another machine. This can be achieved by using Windows File Replication Service or by running programmed scripts. It also helps in updating the previously stored backup copy. Once the full backup is taken, only modified data must be updated in the backup. This can be done with the help of the archive bit. This is not feasible in every situation, because there can be a time lag between two backups.

Archiving

Archiving involves copying user files for future reference. This keeps a permanent record of every version of files created by users. When archived systems fail, they can be restored or rebuilt from the original sources and an archived copy. This is very useful when the system fails due to application failure or when user data gets corrupted. Windows Shadow Copy is an example of this method.

Backup involves copying user and system files to be used when the whole system fails. Tapes can have backups, but they cannot be archived.

File synchronization is the process of updating files stored at different locations with the newest changes to those files. This only works if the files do not change on both ends at the same time.

Both the backup and archive processes are exclusive, and their implementation depends on the nature of the information.

Circuit Redundancy

Circuit redundancy can be implemented by configuring additional data circuits from Internet service providers, and using routing protocols and configured redundant routers. The most used routing protocols are Interior Gateway Routing Protocol (IGRP) and Exterior Gateway Routing Protocol (EGRP). Both of these are link-state protocols and are constantly verifying the state of a route connection with alternative routes stored in the memory.

IGRP factors weight mathematical values for networking delay, bandwidth, and reliability when determining the route to take. It is a stable protocol with features like hold-downs, split horizons, and poison-reverse updates.

EGRP is an extended distance-vectoring routing protocol. It is more widely used than IGRP and factors bandwidth, hop count, maximum packet size, reliability, and traffic load metrics to decide the best possible route. They help in tracing circuit failure and manage routing of data. Multiple circuits can be configured to load-balance traffic and boost bandwidth capacity.

Circuit redundancy requires complex router configuration for effective performance.

Deployment Testing

Deployment testing is used to test software compatibility and catch errors before deploying new software configurations. A test server is created by making a clone of an existing server, and software is installed on that test server. If anything goes wrong on the test server, the error can be corrected before it affects other systems.

Commonly used tools used for deployment testing include the following:

- *VMware from VMware Corporation*: VMware has the following features:
  - Platform independent and divides single physical development environment into various platforms
  - Replicates multimodule production environment into virtual machines for testing
  - Splits development among various teams
  - Removes recurring configuration tasks from development and testing cycles
  - Helps in automating many manual-testing sequences
  - Imitates complex network applications on a single physical platform
- *Virtual PC from Microsoft*: Microsoft Virtual PC is a tool for software virtualization. It helps in executing multiple PC-based operating systems concurrently on one system. This helps in maintaining compatibility with legacy systems and saves reconfiguration time when migrating to a new operating system.

Chapter Summary

- Fault tolerance is the capability of a system to recover from any unpredicted hardware, software, or power failures.

- Systems can fail for any number of reasons, including crime, user error, the environment, and routine events.

- Backups are a general form of fault tolerance and are very important in recovering from any type of failure.

- Uninterruptible power supplies (UPSs) are battery systems that provide continued power during a power failure.

- Physical security measures include locks on entrances, security guards, and video surveillance.

- Offsite storage is the process of sending data to another location so that if anything catastrophic occurs at the original system, the backups or archives are not damaged.

- Redundant Array of Independent Disks, or RAID, describes multiple disks combined into a single logical volume. There are six levels of RAID: 0–5.

- Clustering involves running a single application on multiple machines simultaneously.

Review Questions

1. How is fault tolerance created?

2. What are some fault-tolerance plans?

3. What are some causes of network failure?

4. What are some causes of system failures?

5. What is a backup?

_____

_____

_____

_____

6. What are the functions of UPSs and power generators?

_____

_____

_____

_____

7. What is perimeter security?

_____

_____

_____

_____

8. What is RAID?

_____

_____

_____

_____

9. What are the RAID levels?

_____

_____

_____

_____

10. What is a clustered server?

_____

_____

_____

_____

11. What is simple server redundancy?

_____

_____

_____

Hands-On Projects

1. Read an introduction to fault tolerance.
   - Navigate to Chapter 5 of the Student Resource Center.
   - Open Introduction to Fault Tolerance.pdf and read the content.
2. Read about RAID.
   - Navigate to Chapter 5 of the Student Resource Center.
   - Open RAID.pdf and read the content.

Chapter 6

Incident Response

Objectives

After completing this chapter, you should be able to:

- Classify incidents
- Report incidents
- Manage incidents
- Understand the six-step approach for incident handling
- Understand services provided by incident response teams
- Understand the incident response team life cycle

Key Terms

artifact   any file or tool that is responsible for compromising a system

Introduction to Incident Response

An incident is any event that adversely affects the security of computer systems and networks. This can include a security breach from a hacker, a natural event like a fire or flood, or a power failure. This chapter teaches you how to recognize, report, and respond to incidents in order to minimize damage and resume normal operations.

Classification of Incidents

Incidents can be classified into four different categories based on severity. There are also several different types of incidents.

Categories

- *Category 1*: All the incidents that normally do not affect systems and are not necessarily attacks are placed under category 1, including:
  - Scans and pings from any external, uncontrolled system
  - Virus and Trojan attacks detected and cleared before causing any damage
  - Unauthorized access of information by employees
- *Category 2*: All incidents of potential attacks detected before causing any harm are categorized as category 2 incidents. Some examples of category 2 incidents are:
  - Scans and pings that occur repetitively from unauthorized systems
  - Scanning and mapping of ports by an external network or system
  - Unsuccessful attacks aimed at accessing information without proper authorization
  - Failed DoS or DDoS attacks
  - All harmful spyware, Trojans, and viruses contained in a system
- *Category 3*: Category 3 incidents are successful attempts to damage networks, systems, or information. Although they are successful in causing some damage, the damage is not severe. Examples of category 3 incidents include:
  - Altering or deleting files from Web servers
  - Bypassing firewalls without passing an authorization test
  - Pranks and hoaxes
  - Allowing unauthorized access to important information such as account details and personal information
  - Uncontrolled Trojans, viruses, and spyware
  - Attacks on network services and systems such as NIS, DNS, NFS, e-mail servers, and Web servers
  - Modifications to access privileges
  - Changing the hardware and software configuration of the network
- *Category 4*: All incidents that critically paralyze the system are category 4 incidents. These incidents require the immediate attention of crisis management teams.

Types of Incidents

- *Confidentiality-, integrity-, and availability-related incidents*: In these types of incidents, attackers try to break the security and confidentiality of information in order to modify or delete it. These incidents enable the attacker to carry out DoS attacks.
- *Reconnaissance attacks*: Reconnaissance attacks attempt to gather critical system information for a future attack.
- *Repudiation*: In repudiation incidents, attackers impersonate an authorized person and utilize his or her privileges.
- *Harassments*: In harrassments, the attacker frightens, embarrasses, or troubles the victim using repetitive spam mails, messages, or remote screen-write services.
- *Extortion*: In these kinds of incidents, the attacker tries to extort money from a person by stealing his or her personal information.
- *Pornography and pornography trafficking*: These incidents involve trading pornography on company systems, which can include illegal materials such as child pornography.
- *Organized-crime activities*: These incidents include organized crimes such as trafficking, fraud, and gambling.
- *Subversion*: In subversion incidents, attackers offer applications that seem useful but actually cause damage.
- *Hoaxes*: These incidents involve spreading incorrect information. Hoaxes can negatively affect the functioning and reputation of a person or organization.

Reporting Incidents

When an incident occurs, it is important that it be reported as soon as possible. Any employee even suspecting an incident should report it immediately.

Contact Personnel

The persons to contact in the event of an incident vary according to the functional model of the organization. In general, the following people should be contacted:

- *Site security coordinator*: Site security coordinators monitor compliance with the security policies of the organization and monitor all communication between FedCIRC, incident response teams, and law enforcement agencies.

- *Organizational CSIRT*: A CSIRT, or Computer Security Incident Response Team, is responsible for receiving, reviewing, and responding to computer security incidents and reports. CSIRTs provide their services to corporations, educational organizations, or governments of any region or country. Almost all organizations have a CSIRT for preventing and responding to incidents.

- *FedCIRC*: FedCIRC collects reports of security issues from all sites. FedCIRC should be included in all communications between different sites of the organization and CSIRTs according to the organization's security policies. Contact information is available on the FedCIRC Web site.

- *Law enforcement*: Law enforcement agencies should be contacted so they can take action against attackers.

What to Report

A user who finds an incident should report the following:

- Intensity of the security breach
- Circumstances that revealed the vulnerability
- Shortcomings in design that may have led to the weakness
- Logs showing the intruder's activity
- Specific help needed
- Exact time of the incident

Step-By-Step Procedure

1. *Establish general procedures for responding to incidents*: A CSIRT should be formed and made responsible for managing security incidents. The CSIRT team should be made up of experts from different fields and should be able to manage different sites and different tasks. The roles of each person on the team should be clearly defined.

2. *Prepare to respond to incidents*: The CSIRT team should always be ready to detect any security threat and take the appropriate steps to minimize losses. It should prepare detailed procedures before incidents occur.

3. *Analyze all available information to characterize an incident*: A proper analysis should be done to understand possible incidents and their nature. All incidents should be properly recorded on the information systems administrator's incident reporting form.

4. *Communicate with all parties affected by the incident*: All parties affected by the incident, including administrators, managers, user security enforcement teams, law implementation agencies, and the CERT Coordination Center, should be familiar with the incident response process.

5. *Collect and protect information associated with the incident*: All evidence related to the incident should be properly recorded. Avoid altering the evidence in any way. Make backup copies of the evidence.

6. *Apply short-term solutions to the incident*: The attacked host should be isolated from the network and all accounts should be disabled. Access to the compromised files and shared databases should be restricted.

7. *Eliminate vulnerabilities pertaining to the incident*: The CSIRT team should scan the operating systems and configuration files to detect any kind of attack and undo any changes the attackers made.

8. *Return systems to normal operation*: All systems should be restored to normal so that operations can continue.

9. *Identify and implement security lessons*: Lessons from previous incident responses are very helpful when designing the security process. After an incident is solved, follow these steps:

   - Analyze the incident.
   - Report to senior management.
   - Revise the security plans and procedures.
   - Analyze new risks.
   - Prepare a new inventory of the system and network assets if any changes were made.

10. *Participate in investigation of the sites affected by the incident*: All other sites affected by the incident should be contacted to coordinate the countermeasures for that incident.

Figure 6-1 shows this procedure.

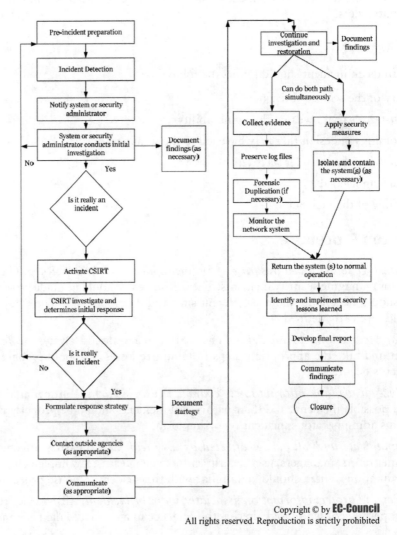

Figure 6-1 This flowchart shows the step-by-step incident response process.

Incident Reporting Forms

US-CERT is a partnership between the Department of Homeland Security and both the public and private sectors. It coordinates defense and responses against cyber attacks across the United States. Figure 6-2 shows the US-CERT incident reporting form, and Figure 6-3 shows the incident reporting form for the CERT Coordination Center.

Contact Information

This section requests information about you and your organization. Please provide as much information as possible. We will keep your identifying information confidential, for use only within the US-CERT unless you *explicitly* authorized this information to be released in the previous section.

Does this report involve U.S. Government Federal Civilian Systems?
○ Yes   ○ No

Reporter's Contact Information

First Name

Last Name

Organization name

Job Title

Email Address

Telephone number? help

From what country are you making this report? *(Required)*   United States

From what time zone are you making this report?   (GMT-05:00) Eastern Time (US & Canada)
(Unless otherwise indicated this response will be used for all times reported in this incident)
(Required)

With what sector are you affiliated? *(Required)*   Select a sector

Please provide your complete postal mailing address

[Previous] [Next] [Abort]

Source: https://forms.us-cert.gov/report/index.php?SID=7a8a5e73f576cbdbb0f749d163ffb765. Accessed 2004.

Figure 6-2   This is the US-CERT incident reporting form.

```
Your contact and organizational information
1. name....................:
2. organization name........:
3. sector type (such as banking, education, energy or
      public safety)..........:
4. email address............:
5. telephone number.........:
6. other....................:


Affected Machine(s)
(duplicate for each host)
7. hostname and IP..........:
8. timezone.................:
9. purpose or function of the host (please be as specific
      as possible)............:


Source(s) of the Attack
(duplicate for each host)
10. hostname or IP...........:
11. timezone.................:
12. been in contact?.........:

13. Estimated cost of handling
      incident (if known).....:

14. Description of the incident (include dates, methods of
      intrusion, intruder tools involved, software versions
      and patch levels, intruder tool output, details of
      vulnerabilities exploited, source of attack, or any
      other relevant information):
```

Source: http://www.cert.org/reporting/incident_form.txt. Accessed 2004.

Figure 6-3   This is the CERT Coordination Center incident reporting form.

Incident Management

Incident management refers to an overall strategy before and after an incident occurs. The first step for managing and responding to the incident is to assemble the team. Incident management aims to meet the following objectives:

- Human safety
- Preservation and recovery of business data
- Regaining computer and network services
- Minimizing damage to the company's reputation

Surviving Large Incidents

To manage large incidents, team members may need to work a good amount of overtime. Team members may need to work on the incident in shifts, 24/7, for several days.

Assigning Ownership

For every significant incident, ownership should be assigned. The owner is assigned all the responsibilities and work related to the incident and is responsible for seeing the task through to its successful conclusion.

The lead role and alternate roles should be assigned. Both should inform the team manager and other team members about the progress and development of work on the incident.

Preparing Tracking Charts

Tracking charts are prepared for managing multiple incidents in a single database of old incidents. These charts can be extremely useful when new incidents occur. A tracking chart should include the following:

- Incident number
- Type of incident
- Location of occurrence
- Point of contact
- Phone numbers of team members
- Priorities assigned to incidents
- Current status of the incident
- Last updates
- Team lead information
- Alternate lead information

Assigning Priorities to Incidents

Priorities should be assigned to every incident according to its severity. It is recommended to use the four-category model presented earlier in this chapter.

Incident Response Architecture

The incident response architecture shown in Figure 6-4 contains the different elements of the security response system and how they interact with each other.

- *Policy*: At the top of the incident response architecture is policy. The security policies properly define the aim of the incidence response. The policy's position at the top of the pyramid indicates its importance.
- *Technology*: Detection and prevention of incidents such as intrusions, virus attacks, hacking, and spoofing require specific and sophisticated tools. These tools require a significant investment, so they should be chosen carefully.

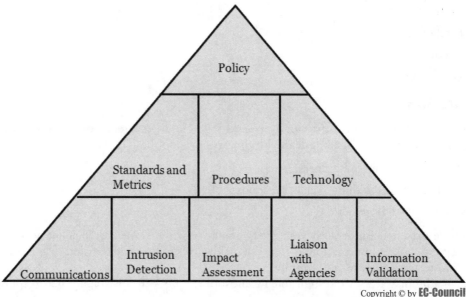

Figure 6-4 This pyramid represents the architecture of incident response.

- *Procedures*: Procedures for the response to any incident should be clearly planned and defined. These procedures have the following benefits:
  - Assistance in training new members
  - Uniform response
  - Quality assurance
  - Legal issues
- *Standards and metrics*: Metrics are mathematical representations of the impact of the incident. These help the management team decide what countermeasures should be taken. Data can include the average time taken for incident detection, average time taken for overcoming the incident, and other details of the nature of the incident.
- *Communication*: Proper communication among the different teams responsible for incident response is extremely important.
- *Intrusion detection*: Timely intrusion detection helps minimize loss.
- *Impact assessment*: Assessing the impact of the incident helps to provide corrective measures and the resources required to restore the system to its original form.
- *Liaisons with agencies*: Agreements with different alert and response agencies help organizations detect attacks and stay informed about new security issues.
- *Information validation*: Information validation mechanisms can help avoid incidents due to hoaxes and tricks.

Six-Step Approach to Incident Handling

Incident handling includes three basic functions:

1. Incident reporting
2. Incident analysis
3. Incident response

The invitational workshop on incident response in Pittsburgh, Pennsylvania, developed the six-step approach for incident handling at the Software Engineering Institute in 1989. This process is still used today. The six steps are:

1. Preparation
2. Detection

3. Containment

4. Eradication

5. Recovery

6. Follow-up

Preparation

Preparation is the readiness to respond prior to the actual occurrence of an event. Methods of dealing with incidents should be established to deal with threats posed to the following:

- Open systems that are vulnerable to attacks
- Secured systems with no incident response
- Systems yet to be secured

It is necessary to define exactly what every employee will do when an incident occurs. Everyone should have the necessary contact information to alert the incident response team. Several resources are required, including special hardware, software, and training.

System administrators are responsible for most of the work in this stage. Their responsibilities include:

- Ensuring password policies are followed
- Disabling default accounts
- Configuring appropriate security mechanisms
- Executing and enabling system logging and auditing
- Managing patches
- Ensuring proper backups
- Ensuring the integrity of file systems
- Identifying abnormal system behavior

Detection

Detection is the identification of malicious code, unauthorized file modifications, or any other incident. Intrusion detection systems (IDS) help identify unauthorized access, but the detection stage involves much more than that.

Detection Software

To effectively detect incidents, software such as IDS, antivirus software, and integrity-checking software is required and should be kept updated. On the other hand, some incidents are noticeable without software. Any of the following conditions could indicate an incident:

- Failing to log in after multiple attempts
- History of activities during non–working hours of the day
- New accounts or unknown files and programs
- Manipulations in configurations
- Extension of user privileges
- Altered Web pages
- Altered system logs
- Suspicious log entries
- Decrease in system speed or system crashes
- Modification of DNS tables, firewalls, or routers

Social Engineering Attempts

Social engineering can result in unauthorized access to the system. Any suspicious activity, however small, should be considered serious. Certain things can indicate social engineering, such as multiple login attempts.

These activities should be constantly monitored, and security awareness training should be regularly provided to all employees.

Initial Actions and Reactions

Once an abnormality is detected, the next steps depend on the specific problem. The response team should start by doing the following tasks:

- Analyzing every anomaly found
- Auditing anomalies and maintaining a copy of compromised files for analysis
- Documenting as much as possible about the incident

Estimating the Scope of an Incident

An incident's scope should be estimated in order to determine the proper procedure and its priority. Scope can be determined by considering the following:

- Number of compromised systems
- Number of networks involved
- How much of the network is affected
- Privileges attacked
- Risk involved
- Number of sources (telephone, fax, PBX, routers, etc.) used while attacking
- Public knowledge of the incident, which affects the organization's reputation

The Reporting Process

A reporting policy should be created and provided to the staff so that there is no delay in incident reporting. The security policy needs to consider, at minimum, the following:

- What should be reported
- The contact who will receive the report
- Method of reporting (e-mail, phone, etc.)
- Consequences of violating policies
- When to notify the legal department, incident response teams, public affairs, etc.

Containment

Once actions in the detection phase lead to the determination that an incident occurred, it is important to contain the incident in order to reduce loss and damage. Different measures should be taken depending on the type of incident. For example, if multiple failed login attempts occur, the logical containment measure is disabling that account.

In the event of an incident, systems should not be shut down without informing the designated authority (e.g., system and network administrators). They may need to observe what is happening before doing anything else.

Once the administrator is made aware of the incident, possible containment strategies include:

- Immediately shutting down the system to avoid attack advancement
- Disconnecting from the network
- Altering filtering rules of network devices to reject data from unknown hosts
- Enhanced monitoring of network activities
- Setting traps for attackers
- Disabling file transfer services to stop vulnerabilities
- Observing and noting the course of the incident

Fingerprints and backdoors that allow attackers to communicate with the system have to be identified and removed, but records must be kept to legally prove that an attack has occurred. Changing passwords is often not enough to prevent unauthorized access.

Eradication

Once the incident is contained, the original cause of the incident must be eradicated to prevent its return. Backups should be scanned and cleared of malicious code, and antivirus software should be run. In certain cases involving high security, the physical media must be completely destroyed. The incident response team needs to do the following:

- Adhere to eradication procedures
- Advise users to report the status of compromised systems constantly
- Apply updates and patches
- Decide how much about the incident should be disclosed to outsiders

Recovery

In the recovery stage, systems and devices are returned to a normal operating state. Recovering a system by restoring backups using good media is one of the best recovery methods, although it can be time consuming. Every access credential and password should be restored.

In this stage, the team must do the following:

- Document all events carefully
- Keep track of the status of compromised systems
- Use systems only after they are completely recovered
- Adhere to defined policies
- Log system activities

After recovery, the team should return network filtering rules to normal.

Follow-Up

Follow-up activity is necessary for the following reasons:

- It improves the skills of those involved in incident response.
- It provides proof of performance.
- It helps the team avoid repeating mistakes in the future.
- It helps team development.
- It provides information for legal proceedings.

The follow-up report should be as complete as possible, using information documented in earlier steps. It helps in evaluating the incident response procedures, identifying gaps, and updating them accordingly. It is also crucial in estimating the amount of damage caused.

Performing a Cost Analysis

Cost analysis can also help in determining the budget necessary for future security efforts. Costs include the following:

- Tangible, quantifiable costs
  - Cost to establish the incident
  - Lost data
  - Damaged hardware
  - Lost productivity hours
  - Investigation and recovery efforts
  - Loss of business
  - Loss or theft of resources

- Intangible costs
  - Damage to corporate reputation
  - Loss of goodwill
  - Morale damage
  - Legal liability
  - Effect on shareholder value

Document the Quality of the Response

The following questions should be asked to determine the quality of the response:

- Was the incident detected promptly? Why or why not?
- Could virus eradication and detection tools prevent future incidents?
- Was there sufficient containment of the incident?
- What particular difficulties were encountered?
- Was there sufficient preparation for the incident?
- Were the necessary procedures communicated properly?

Computer Security Incident Response Team (CSIRT)

A computer security incident response team, or CSIRT, is responsible for the planning and execution of measures to be taken in the case of an incident. It is made up of security specialists who conduct expanded research programs about security concerns, leading to advancements in the organization's computer security.

Incident response efforts should be assigned to specific team or contractor. The CSIRT can be either in-house or outsourced.

Outsourcing can be a cost-effective measure because an external team will just deal with incidents as they take place. If there are few incidents, a full-time team is an unnecessary cost. Professional consultants have a great amount of experience in that specific field and use the most current tools available. Of course, credentials and experience must be checked before entering into a contract.

The main purpose of maintaining an in-house CSIRT is that in-house response teams can better understand the specific organization's security policies. In many cases, sensitive information should not be revealed to a third-party contractor.

Functional Requirements

The functional requirements and role of the CSIRT should be defined early. One option is for the team to have complete control over an incident and any computing and data resources involved, while another is for the team to simply advise users when needed.

Additional requirements include:

- *Interagency coordination*: The response team may coordinate with other teams such as the business continuity organization, law enforcement agencies.
- *Contingency planning and business continuity services*: In some organizations, the incident response team also performs contingency planning and business continuity functions. This helps the team become more skilled in recognizing and dealing with emergencies.
- *Information security tool development*
- *Incident response planning and analysis*: A few teams must analyze trends to plan for incident response and security needs.
- *Training and awareness*: The CSIRT should provide training and awareness programs to help users identify incidents.

Methods of Communication

The response team communicates with each other and its clients using the following:

- Telephone
- E-mail
- Fax
- Bulletins or notices
- Web sites
- Conferences
- Workshops
- Media interviews
- Instructional videos

Staffing Issues

When staffing the CSIRT, the first thing that should be considered is the size of the team. Team size is determined mainly by the budget allocated for the CSIRT. At minimum, it is necessary to have one person lead the team and a secondary technical expert.

Team members must have the following skills:

- *Management skills*: The manager should perform the following tasks:
  - Ensure that the team has the necessary skills for the task
  - Organize and coordinate the team's activities
  - Motivate and keep team members on track
  - Ensure proper priorities, procedures, and policies
  - Prepare reports for management
  - Monitors the team's work
- *Technical skills*: For the response team to be effective, technical skills are essential. Sound knowledge of network security issues and methods is required.
- *People skills*: The team must be able to work with clients as smoothly as possible.
- *Teamwork skills*: The team must function well together, which can be difficult for many people.
- *Communication skills*: Communication skills include both interpersonal skills and teamwork skills. For more effective communication, many companies hire a technical writer. A technical writer can produce accurate and understandable bulletins and notices.

Incident Response Team Life Cycle

An incident response team has a four-stage life cycle:

1. *Initial*: In the initial stage, management has accepted and approved the creation of the team.
2. *Critical*: In the critical stage, the incident response team is formed. The requirements and objectives of the team are finalized and approved by management. This is called the critical stage because it decides the success of the team, so everything must be done with great care.
3. *Established*: In this stage, the team settles into efficient operations and learns to effectively handle incidents. Management can see the work of the team and form communication channels.
4. *Postestablished*: After the establishment of operations, the team can grow and expand its operations.

Obstacles in Building a Successful Response Team

An incident response team may run into the following obstacles:

- *Budget*: Lack of funding or mismanagement of the budget can make operations difficult.
- *Management reluctance*: It is the responsibility of team leaders to meet with managers regularly and submit their reports. If management is not on board, it can become difficult to function properly.

- *Organizational resistance*: Other employees, in particular IT personnel, may be reluctant to cooperate with the CSIRT.
- *Politics*: Interpersonal politics can cause obstacles in the organizational process.
- *User awareness*: Users must be knowledgeable about basic security practices such as password choices.
- *External coordination*: For a response team to be effective, an external source should monitor the incident. Effective coordination with these external teams is very important.
- *Law enforcement*: Sometimes, law enforcement agencies must be involved to address issues of whether or not to take legal action against those responsible for incidents.
- *Media*: Negative media attention can cause significant damage to the organization's reputation.

Services Provided

CSIRT services can be divided into three categories:

1. Reactive services
2. Proactive services
3. Security quality management services

Reactive Services

Reactive services are direct responses to appeals for assistance and reported incidents. This includes:

- Distributing alerts and warnings
- Incident handling
- Incident analysis
- Vulnerability handling
- Artifact handling

In this context, an *artifact* is any file or tool that is responsible for compromising a system. Artifacts must be identified, analyzed, and removed.

Proactive Services

Proactive services improve security by preventing incidents from taking place and taking steps to minimize damage before it happens. Proactive services include the following:

- Sending announcements about new attacks
- Watching developments in technology
- Security audits or assessments
  - Infrastructure review
  - Standards review
  - Vulnerability scanning
  - Penetration testing
- Arrangement and maintenance of security tools, applications, infrastructures, and services
  - Developing security tools
  - Implementing intrusion detection systems (IDS) and reviewing IDS logs
- Security-related information dissemination
  - Compiling reports of guidelines and contact information
  - Archiving alerts and warnings
  - Documenting existing standards and practices
  - Security guidance
  - Security and methodologies

- Patch management
- Current statistics
- Incident reporting
- Artifact response coordination with vendors, researchers, and security professionals

Security Quality Management Services

After obtaining experience with reactive and proactive services, a CSIRT can provide security quality management services based on that experience. These services include:

- Risk analysis
- Business continuity and disaster recovery planning
- Security consulting
- Awareness building
- Product evaluation or certification

Chapter Summary

- An incident is any event that adversely affects the security of computer systems and networks.
- Incidents can be classified into four different categories based on severity.
- The persons to contact in the event of an incident vary according to the functional model of the organization.
- US-CERT is a partnership between the Department of Homeland Security and both the public and private sectors.
- Incident handling includes three basic functions: incident reporting, incident analysis, and incident response.
- A computer security incident response team, or CSIRT, is responsible for the planning and execution of measures to be taken in the case of an incident.

Review Questions

1. What are the categories of incidents?

   _____

   _____

   _____

   _____

2. What are the types of incidents?

   _____

   _____

   _____

   _____

3. How should an incident be reported?

   _____

   _____

   _____

   _____

4. How are priorities assigned to incidents?

5. What are the six steps for handling incidents?

6. What is a CSIRT?

7. What services are performed by a CSIRT?

8. What are the functional requirements of a CSIRT?

9. What are some obstacles that can occur when building a CSIRT?

10. What are reactive services?

11. What are proactive services?

_____

_____

_____

_____

Hands-On Projects

1. Use the EASEUS Deleted File Recovery tool to recover deleted files.

   ■ Navigate to Chapter 6 of the Student Resource Center.

   ■ Install and launch the EASEUS Deleted File Recovery program.

   ■ Click **Option** to view the list of options available for NTFS allocation.

   ■ Click **NTFS.**

   ■ Select a partition and click **Next.**

   ■ The program will generate a list of files deleted. Select some files and click **Next** to recover the deleted files.

   ■ Select a path to which the recovered files will be saved and click **Next.**

2. Use the PC Inspector Smart Recovery tool to recover deleted pictures, videos, or sound files from the selected media.

   ■ Navigate to Chapter 6 of the Student Resource Center.

   ■ Install and launch the PC Inspector Smart Recovery program.

   ■ Click **File** and then **Settings.**

   ■ Change the search method to **Intensive Mode** and set the file recovery size limit.

   ■ Set the options for device, format type, and destination folder.

   ■ Click **Start** to run the application.

   ■ The list of files found can be viewed under **Progress.**

3. Read about computer security incident handling.

   ■ Navigate to Chapter 6 of the Student Resource Center.

   ■ Open Computer Security Incident Handling.pdf and read the content.

4. Read about CSIRT planning.

   ■ Navigate to Chapter 6 of the Student Resource Center.

   ■ Open csirplanning.pdf and read the content.

5. Read about CSIRTs.

   ■ Navigate to Chapter 6 of the Student Resource Center.

   ■ Open Computer Security Incident Response Teams.pdf and read the content.

Chapter 7

Disaster Recovery Planning and Risk Analysis

Objectives

After completing this chapter, you should be able to:

- Understand the principles of disaster recovery
- Plan for disaster recovery
- Understand disaster recovery testing
- Understand risk analysis
- Understand the business continuity planning process
- Understand business continuity management
- Prevent disasters

Key Terms

Business continuity planning   the detailed logistical planning of how an organization will restore interrupted critical functions within a specified time after a partial or total disruption of its operations

Business impact analysis   a risk analysis process that involves identifying the critical business functions within an organization and determining the impact of losing those business functions beyond the maximum acceptable outage

Introduction to Disaster Recovery Planning and Risk Analysis

A disaster is any event, natural or man-made, that threatens human safety or computer system availability. Disasters are often unpredictable, so it is important to prepare for them ahead of time in order to quickly recover. This chapter teaches you how to plan and execute effective disaster recovery, as well as to analyze risk.

Disaster Recovery Overview

When planning for disaster recovery, the first step is to assess the organization's risks. This involves designing, documenting, implementing, testing, and maintaining procedures to minimize losses after a disaster. This is a part of *business continuity planning*, which is a detailed logistical planning of how an organization will restore interrupted critical functions within a specified time after a partial or total disruption of its operations.

Issues such as hackers, computer viruses, and an increased dependence on computers have all led to a greater focus on disaster recovery planning. Prior to forming a disaster recovery plan, it is necessary to analyze the whole business continuity plan and perform a business impact analysis to determine the effects a disaster may have.

Any disaster, from floods and fires to viruses and cyber terrorism, can influence the accessibility, authenticity, and privacy of critical business resources, which can be devastating to any business.

Disaster recovery plans, also called contingency plans, include the employment of interchange sites (hot, warm, and cold sites), redundant data centers, disaster insurance, business impact analysis, and authorized accountabilities.

Principles of Disaster Recovery

A disaster recovery plan should identify the size of the organization along with characteristics including vital resources and the number of employees. A sequential process should be developed describing all disaster recovery elements.

Disaster recovery plans require the support of management, legal counsel, and the directors of individual departments such as human resources, resource management, IT, and corporate security. They require detailed analysis of environmental, economic, and social conditions.

The policies of the disaster recovery plan should address the needs of the business operation with specific rules and regulations. These rules must be certified by management and must be clear to the executing team. The plan defines the hierarchy of managers who are in charge of declaring, reacting to, and recovering from a disaster. The flow must also specify the roles of internal and external departments involved in disaster recovery, permitting interactions among decision makers, managers, and staff along with outside parties such as law enforcement, emergency services, and the media. Employees must be trained to execute their assigned actions and to locate unexpected problems.

Procedures must be tested to identify any vulnerabilities in the plan. If any are discovered, the plan, procedures, or training must be updated. New threats and business conditions can also require further updates to the plan, so it should be regularly revisited and tested.

Business Process Inventory

A business process inventory lists key business processes required to manage operations. These processes must be restored in the event of a disaster. It includes the following information:

- How the process works
- Occurrences of the process
- Performance of the process
- People involved
- Equipment used
- Tasks the process is required to accomplish

Backups

A backup is a copy of important data that can be referenced if anything happens to the original data. There are several methods for backing up data, including:

- Full backup, when all data is completely copied file-by-file
- Image or volume backup, when the data is copied bit-by-bit
- Incremental backup, when files updated since the last backup are copied
- Mirroring, when changes are made to the backup and original data at the same time

The backup process is also known as *data synchronization*.

Synchronous Systems

Synchronous systems, also known as *two-stage commit systems*, ensure that no I/O contract can be dedicated to the disk of the primary system, unless it has also been dedicated to the disk of the support system. The majority of these systems are hardware dependent and engage attached storage, such as NAS or SAN systems, but there are also software-based synchronous systems.

When an I/O request is started on the main system, that request is sent to the support system first. After the request is confirmed by the backup system, the I/O is dedicated to the primary disk system. This guarantees that all changes on the primary system are also mirrored on the backup.

Although synchronous approaches provide outstanding data security and guarantee that both disk systems are the same at all times, they have several disadvantages. These systems are usually much more costly than asynchronous systems. Additionally, due to the nature of the two-phase commit technology, I/O reply time is much slower. Synchronous systems are highly impractical unless both systems are physically located very close to one another, which can render them useless when recovering from a natural disaster like a fire or flood.

Asynchronous Systems

Asynchronous disaster recovery systems are commonly software based and reside on the host server rather than on the attached storage array. I/O requests are committed to the primary disk system immediately, while a copy of that I/O is sent to the backup disk systems. Asynchronous systems can send a continuous stream of I/O data to the backup systems without slowing down I/O response time on the primary system.

Asynchronous systems have technology to make sure that if something is lost in transmission, it can be resent, so it is very practical to use with TCP/IP and off-site backup systems. The main disadvantage of this system is that a few transactions may be lost at the time of a failover event. If the primary server suddenly goes offline, anything waiting to be transmitted to the backup system will be lost.

Backup Sites

When the primary operations center is compromised, it is important to have a site from which the recovery can take place. This is known as the backup site. There are three different types of backup sites:

1. *Cold backup sites* are simply a suitably configured room in a building. Everything necessary to restore service is sent to this site before recovery can begin.

2. *Warm backup sites* have an exact copy of the hardware found in the main data center.

3. *Hot backup sites* have a practical reflection of the hardware in the current data center, with all computers configured similarly, so all they need is the most recent data backup to get up and running.

Backup sites can come from three different sources:

1. Third parties that offer disaster recovery services

2. Other locations

3. A shared facility with another organization

Designing an agreement to share data centers with another company can be costly and time consuming.

Small-System Recovery

Desktop PCs and laptops are networked to other devices, applications, and the Internet. To recover small systems when a disaster occurs, the organization should do the following:

- Train users to keep a backup of all data
- Store backup media off-site
- Allow only standardized hardware and software components

System configurations must be properly documented, including vendor details with emergency contact information, in case a replacement is needed.

Large-System Recovery

Large systems contain file servers, application servers, Web servers, and mainframes. Efforts to recover them include:

- Uninterruptible power supplies
- Replication of addresses
- Fault-tolerant network systems

Redundant, critical system components utilize RAID (Redundant Array of Independent Disks). This ensures data availability by keeping redundant data across multiple disk drives, although the system will see a RAID as a single drive. Some forms of RAID use a parity technique to identify lost data or overwritten data.

Network Recovery

Detailed documentation is essential to rebuilding damaged networks. Services that help to reduce network downtime include:

- Redundant communication links
- Multiple network service contributors
- Network security systems
- IDS and IPS

Disaster Recovery Planning

Disaster recovery planning is necessary to guarantee permanence of operations. Prior to the formation of a disaster recovery plan, it is necessary to analyze the whole business continuity plan and judge the possible impact of a disaster.

Security Planning

The planning made to manage or reduce risk is called security planning. Components of security planning include:

- *Risk analysis*: This determines the level of risk and checks for further vulnerabilities in order to reduce that risk. It includes both qualitative analysis and quantitative analysis.
- *Roles and responsibilities*: Different people have different roles and responsibilities. For example, the chief security officer has to take complete responsibility for the security process, and the network manager has the responsibility of maintaining passwords.
- *System configuration*: System configuration checks:
  - Whether the systems can interact with one another
  - Whether the systems are configured appropriately
  - Whether the software is appropriate and sufficient
- *Antivirus controls and intrusion detection*: Antivirus controls define the countermeasures to get rid of viruses and worms. This includes antivirus software and maintaining administrative privileges to keep users from installing unauthorized software. Intrusion detection systems alert administrators to the presence of intruders.
- *Physical security*: An organization needs to secure its assets, including both personnel and property.
- *Network security*: This defines who can access which resources.
- *Data access*: It is important to distinguish restricted data from unrestricted data. Restricted data is further classified into data with read-only access and data with read and modification access.
- *Outsourcing*: This specifies the security provided to outsourced services.
- *Policies and procedures*: Policies and procedures must be carefully and completely documented.
- *Team planning*: Teams should be planned in accordance with the size and complexity of the organization. As the complexity of the organization increases, the team size should also increase.

Budget Planning

Disasters are difficult to measure in the IT industry, so it can be challenging to set a security and recovery budget. It is important that the plan be suitable for the long term; thus, it should be budgeted with long-term planning in mind instead of designing the budget layout with only present conditions.

Guidelines for budget planning include:

- *Existing security*: Use familiar and built-in security mechanisms to help attain reliable security.
- *Prior planning*: A secure environment should have the following characteristics:
  - A staff that is aware of the security measures
  - A well-performing network
  - Carefully documented policies and procedures
  - Centralized monitoring and altering
- *Experts*: In some cases, it is necessary to hire a third-party expert to assist in planning. These experts have specialized knowledge and experience to perform the necessary tasks.

Disaster Recovery Planning Process

The first step in the disaster recovery process is to execute a business impact examination that considers all of the possible impacts of a disaster. Disaster recovery plans should cover how to deal with at least these events:

- Natural catastrophes (e.g., earthquake, fire, flood, storm)
- Terrorist attacks
- Power failure
- Computer software or hardware loss
- Computer shutdowns due to hackers, viruses, etc.
- Processing shutdowns
- Labor strikes

The process of creating a disaster recovery plan is as follows:

1. *Establish a disaster recovery planning team*: This requires a high-level team leader designated by the CEO for effective planning. Each department must have a representative and an alternate, in case the primary representative is unavailable at any time. When the team is ready, activities are scheduled, specifying the time of the meeting and the completion of the work. Fixed schedules are important to complete the project on time.

2. *Perform a business impact analysis to assess risks*: A business impact analysis is used to assess any potential losses. Reviews are done on the type of threat involved and the related insurance required.

3. *Assign responsibilities in the departments and organization*: The disaster recovery planning team allocates work to every member of the company, including management, staff, business partners, and outside service organizations. The coordinator plays the lead role here. Managers of different departments need to assign the work to their employees. The coordinator also decides which department should do which work in disaster recovery.

4. *Develop policies and procedures*: These policies are the guiding principles for the development of disaster recovery procedures. Procedures are the step-by-step techniques intended to restore an organizational function or business process.

5. *Document disaster recovery procedures*: This documentation includes drafting, reviewing, and approving policies and procedures. This approved documentation is added to the disaster recovery plan.

6. *Distribute the plan*: In this step, the final approved plan is distributed to all the departments, organizations, and employees involved in the disaster recovery plan.

7. *Implement training, testing, and rehearsal of the plan*: The plan must be tested and training must be provided to everyone in the organization, including executives, middle managers, supervisors, and all employees. The disaster response team should also be trained in the event of an emergency.

8. *Ongoing management*: After the plan is implemented and tested, the planning team must evaluate new threats, assess the scalability of the program, and determine the impact of new technologies on recovery procedures.

Organizing

Work must be delegated to team members. Every department in the organization should be represented by two people. The primary representative acts as the full member of the planning team, while the alternate representative works as a secondary member in the team.

Each member of the team has specific roles and responsibilities. The following are some of the more important roles:

- *IT and network manager*: IT and network departments require more representatives, because the main function of these departments is to provide help by assessing business functions, including the procedure to switch to backup computer systems and networks. They should address enterprise issues as well as specific department and business application issues.

- *Interdepartmental subcommittees*: A disaster recovery team forms subcommittees for special planning issues. These committees include planning team members and technical experts from various departments. The major responsibility of these groups is to solve specific problems and explore the unique planning issues of different departments.

- *Departmental-level team*: The department planning team should consider disaster recovery issues at a departmental level. These teams research their specific departments to help establish, evaluate, and implement a corporate plan.

- *Executive champions*: The role of an executive champion is to express the importance of the disaster recovery planning team across the organization.

Training

After organizing the disaster recovery planning team, the next step is to provide training to team members. Every member in the team should research disaster recovery issues that affect their disciplines or departments. This research must include:

- Case studies of other organizations' work
- Professional papers
- Government regulations

Generally, training is provided by the organization itself, but sometimes it is necessary to employ outside assistance. Once an organization completes its initial training, it can search for outside help to fill in any gaps. For example, if any company does not have in-house legal counsel, then it needs trained policy and procedure writers.

For a team to work together effectively within the allotted time, it is necessary to make a schedule. Regular meetings should be scheduled first, and then weekly meetings should be planned. The team coordinator has the responsibility of overseeing the scheduling of every meeting. The communication channel among members must be established in the initial meetings. However, it is sometimes not possible to gather all members together at the same time.

Implementing

The next step is the implementation of the plan. This implementation affects all of the departments in the organization, so its progress should be checked regularly. The following are the steps that are carried out to implement the plan:

- *Assigning responsibilities*: The coordinator of the disaster recovery plan assigns work to each team member. The coordinator plays the lead role in monitoring and evaluating the progress of the implementation. Managers of different departments assign work to their employees. The coordinator also decides which department should do which work in disaster recovery.

- *Establishing a schedule*: The coordinator of the disaster recovery plan designs the time schedule of the implementation plan to ensure the completion of activities within a specific time frame.

The speed of the activities depends on available resources and the efficiency of employees. The coordinator and planning team should check the progress of implementation by compiling monthly reports from departments.

- *Distributing disaster recovery documentation*: Disaster recovery plan documents must be available to all the members during implementation and testing. These documents include written analyses, policies, and procedures that should be followed by employees in the case of a disaster. Distribution methods include company intranet, hosted Web server, digital copies, and paper copies.

- *Evaluating the worth and efficiency of mitigation steps*: It is important for the team to recognize if the steps taken are the most efficient ways to prevent disasters; it is also necessary for management to decide if the cost is worth the reduction in risk.

- *Administering internal and external knowledge campaigns*: Knowledge campaigns are carried out using the present channels of communication and by training employees, customers, and business partners.

- *Implementing training programs for disaster recovery*: Training must be provided for executives, middle managers, supervisors, disaster response teams, and employees.

Testing

Disaster recovery plans can be tested in the following ways:

- Procedure audits verify that data are correct, the right hardware is installed, and everything is properly staffed.

- A live walkthrough of the procedures checks efficiency by testing that everything is working properly and producing the correct results. Related procedures should also be checked during the live walkthrough.

- Scenario testing establishes a mock disaster, such as a fire, to ensure that the procedures for handling that disaster are effective.

- Workgroup-, department-, and facility-level tests will show how well teams work together in a mock disaster.

- Enterprise-level tests check whether procedures work effectively for the entire organization in a mock disaster.

Procedures must be checked after they are designed, and they should be tested frequently to ensure that the plan is updated with the most current data. Procedure auditors should produce a report determining any necessary changes to the procedures, which will then be handed in to the coordinator.

Testing Scenarios Scenarios must be developed to simulate specific threats and determine the effectiveness of disaster recovery procedures. Scenario testing uses mock disasters such as severe weather or a fire to determine how well the procedures work during these events. The following testing scenarios should be applied:

- *Evacuation and safety exercises*: In the event of dangerous disasters like fires, personnel must be evacuated, so this should be part of the testing process. If organizations deal with hazardous material, controlled substances, valuable items, or rare materials, they must be prepared to implement necessary procedures during evacuation.

- *Testing for special cases*: Organizations develop scenarios for special circumstances, such as:
  - Hazardous elements such as explosives, flammables, and poisons
  - Nonreplaceable items such as art or antiques
  - Trade secrets and proprietary processes

- *Testing for shutdown and lockdown procedures*: These scenarios test shutdown procedures as well as lockdown and security procedures for protecting valuable items and lives. Monitors should observe these tests.

- *Testing emergency service response procedures*: Disaster recovery plans rely on an established working relationship with local emergency service providers. Joint drills and rehearsals of disaster response procedures should be conducted with these service providers.

Risk Analysis

Risk analysis is used to assess the chances of a disaster occurring, and the potential loss due to that event. It is done as a part of disaster recovery planning and as a part of the software development cycle. It also defines procedures through which an organization can survive or reduce the probability of risks.

Risk analysis analyzes the following elements:

- Assets, such as computers, databases, hardware, software, and networks
- Threats, including natural disasters and security threats
- Vulnerabilities
- Losses, such as loss of data, information modification, service delays, or equipment theft
- Safeguards designed to reduce vulnerabilities

The steps involved in risk analysis are:

1. Set parameters for analyzing the threats.
2. Define the assets of the organization.
3. Provide relevant threat profiles with preventive measures.
4. Recognize vulnerabilities.
5. Analyze all available information.
6. Make a report of the analysis.

Potential Threats

Potential threats to be addressed in risk analysis include:

- Natural threats, such as flooding, fire, earthquakes, winds, snow and ice storms, tornadoes, hurricanes, mass illness, tidal waves, and typhoons
- Technical threats, such as power failures, ventilation failure, CPU malfunction, software failure, telecommunications failure, gas leaks, communications failure, and nuclear fallout
- Human threats, such as robbery, embezzlement, extortion, vandalism, terrorism, civil disorder, chemical spill, sabotage, biological contamination, radiation contamination, hazardous waste, vehicle crash, work stoppage, and computer crime

Methods of Risk Analysis

Expected Impact

Impact is commonly represented in terms of the monetary cost of failure. For every requirement or feature, it is possible to assign a value in terms of the expected impact of the failure of that requirement or feature. The team assigns a value of high, medium, or low for each requirement, based on the measure of the expected impact. Figure 7-1 shows an example of an expected impact report.

Login Function		Likelihood	Impact
Requirements	**Attribute**		
User ID's	Minimum of 4 characters	High	Low
Passwords	Minimum of 5 characters	High	Low
System	Validate User ID and Password	High	High
Welcome Screen	Successful Login	Low	Low

Figure 7-1   This is an example of the expected impact and likelihood of failure for the login process.

The *User ID shall be 4 characters* requirement has a low expected impact of failure, because there will not be very much of an impact to a user if the user ID is more or less than four characters.

Likelihood of Failure

The team should assign a value of how likely each requirement or feature is to fail.

Severity

Severity indicates how much damage there will be to the community and the user if the requirement or feature fails. This can include money, emotional stress, poor health, or death. Severity is different from expected impact because expected impact does not consider the suffering imposed on the user.

Complexity

The more decisions a program makes, the more complex it is. Programs or features with higher complexities have more risks.

Figure 7-2 shows the expected impact, likelihood of failure, complexity, and severity of several requirements related to login functionality.

Risk Management

Risk management identifies threats, checks the probability of their occurrence, and provides measures to overcome these threats. It also manages computer security threats by installing better security systems and making personnel aware of the threats.

Risk management includes risk assessment, which is the determination of risk, and risk mitigation, which reduces threats that disturb the routine operations of the organization. These threats can be mitigated by reducing the occurrence of the risk or by reducing the severity of the risk.

The risk management process includes the following five steps, as shown in Figure 7-3:

1. Risks are identified.
2. Risks are assessed.
3. A risk management plan is developed.
4. The developed plan is tested and implemented.
5. Risks are reevaluated.

Information Identification

As part of the risk management process, as much information as possible should be collected about each system. This information can come from the following records:

- Operating manuals
- Reference books

Login Function		Likelihood	Impact	Compl exity	Severity
Requirements	**Attribute**				
User ID's	Minimum of 4 characters	High	Low	Medium	Medium
Passwords	Minimum of 5 characters	High	Low	Medium	Low
System	Validate User ID and Password	High	High	High	High
Welcome Screen	Successful Login	Low	Low	Low	Low

Figure 7-2   This shows the expected impact, likelihood of failure, complexity, and severity for login functionality.

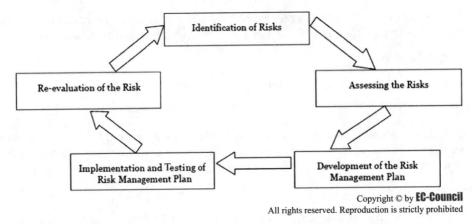

Figure 7-3 These are the five steps in the risk management process.

- Building and safety codes
- Lists of contractors

Roles and Responsibilities in Risk Analysis

Every employee has a specific task in risk analysis. Roles and responsibilities are as follows:

- Chief administrative officer/information resources manager
  - Responsible for the establishment and maintenance of security
  - Establishes the risk management process
  - Ensures information resources for audit requirements and participates with all levels of employees to implement policies and procedures
  - Prepares and maintains the disaster recovery plan for information resources
- Information resources security officer
  - Identifies threats and vulnerabilities
  - Identifies restricted, sensitive, and unrestricted information resources
  - Develops and maintains risk management processes and updated security procedures
- Owner of information resources
  - Assesses information
  - Classifies information according to who can access it
  - Identifies risks
  - Plans contingencies to recover information if a disaster occurs
- Custodian
  - Responsible for physical possession of information resources
  - Implements security controls specified by the owner of information resources
  - Provides safeguards to information resources
  - Provides administrative access to information resources
- Technical management
  - Ensures that technical support is provided
  - Develops and maintains contingency plans
  - Develops procedures to report on monitored controls
- Security administrators
  - Helps other personnel implement the security plan
  - Assists with software or hardware upgrades

- Makes staff aware of vulnerabilities
- Maintains user accounts, passwords, and keys
- Internal auditor
  - Calculates effective security controls
  - Provides security policies, standards, and guidelines
  - Examines planned security controls

Risk Analysis Results Evaluation

Once the risk analysis team has reviewed the results of the risk analysis, they will summarize the results and make suggestions to lessen the risk.

Myths About Disaster Recovery

One Recovery Plan Can Meet All Requirements

In reality, there will be several plans, fitting different scenarios. Different situations require different actions. For example, certain types of disaster recovery involve keeping in touch with legal authorities, while others involve the use of the company's PR department.

The More Distance Between the Primary Site and Backup Site, the Better the Protection

While it is true that a greater distance means that both sites are less likely to be hit by the same disaster, there are other factors as well. Greater distance can lead to greater costs, and it can mean less security when everything is not close together. It increases the risk of damaged links and line failures.

A Combined Approach Must Be Followed to Allow for Business Continuity Planning and Testing

This refers to performing a *business impact analysis* (BIA) when planning for business permanence. This is a risk analysis process that involves identifying the critical business functions within an organization and determining the impact of losing those business functions beyond the maximum acceptable outage.

Three of the most significant deliverables from a BIA are:

1. *Recovery-time objective (RTO)*: The targeted amount of time between when a disaster occurs and when the business process returns to operation
2. *Recovery-point objective (RPO)*: The place in the business process to which data must be restored after a disaster takes place; for example, the beginning of the business day, the most recent backup, or the last processed transaction
3. *Cost of downtime*: The probable losses, both as the result of a disaster and in recovering lost data

Data Recovery Restricts Data Losses to a Minimum

Data reliability must be guaranteed for a speedy recovery. If the data are not reliable at the recovery site, the data will have to be analyzed, or recovery from tape may be required. This could take a long time, which can cause significant losses. It is important that companies completely understand how their selected duplication technology works, what its restrictions are, and how it will respond in different disaster scenarios. Then, a plan can be formulated to guarantee data revival with reliability, while still meeting RPOs.

Maintaining a Copy of Mirrored Data Is Sufficient at Recovery Site

There should be two copies at the recovery site: a main copy and a point-in-time copy. If the remote copy functionality is withheld, a division between the target (secondary disk) and the point-in-time copy should be executed. If a disaster strikes again during the synchronization process, data on the secondary disk may not be stable, but the point-in-time copy will contain the most recent stable image. The local copy is reset after resynchronization is done.

A Large Amount of Bandwidth Is Required for Remote Backups

For synchronous systems, a large amount of bandwidth is required. However, when using asynchronous remote copy, significantly less bandwidth is necessary.

Chapter Summary

- A disaster is any event, natural or man-made, that threatens human safety or computer system availability.
- Disaster recovery plans, also called contingency plans, include the employment of interchange sites (hot, warm, and cold sites), redundant data centers, disaster insurance, business impact analysis, and authorized accountabilities.
- A backup is a copy of important data that can be referenced if anything happens to the original data.
- There are two types of disaster recovery systems: synchronous systems and asynchronous systems.
- The planning made to manage or reduce risk is called security planning.
- Risk analysis is used to assess the chances of a disaster occurring, and the potential loss due to that event.
- Risk management identifies threats, checks the probability of their occurrence, and provides measures to overcome these threats.

Review Questions

1. What are the types of disasters?

   _____

   _____

   _____

   _____

2. What is disaster recovery?

   _____

   _____

   _____

   _____

3. What is the difference between synchronous backup systems and asynchronous backup systems?

   _____

   _____

   _____

   _____

4. What is a disaster recovery plan?

   _____

   _____

   _____

   _____

5. What is the process of disaster recovery planning?

_____

_____

_____

_____

6. What are the roles of a disaster recovery team?

_____

_____

_____

_____

7. Why might outside help be required in training?

_____

_____

_____

_____

8. What are the steps involved in disaster recovery testing?

_____

_____

_____

_____

9. What are testing scenarios?

_____

_____

_____

_____

10. What is risk assessment?

_____

_____

_____

_____

Hands-On Projects

1. Read about disaster recovery planning.

   ▪ Navigate to Chapter 7 of the Student Resource Center.

   ▪ Open DisasterRecoveryPlan.pdf and read the content.

2. Read more about disaster recovery planning.

   ▪ Navigate to Chapter 7 of the Student Resource Center.

   ▪ Open Disaster Recovery Planning.pdf and read the content.

3. Read about practical disaster recovery planning.

   ▪ Navigate to Chapter 7 of the Student Resource Center.

   ▪ Open Practical_Disaster_Recovery_Planning.pdf and read the content.

4. Read about business continuity planning.

   ▪ Navigate to Chapter 7 of the Student Resource Center.

   ▪ Open bus_continuity_plan.pdf and read the content.

5. Read a disaster-planning checklist.

   ▪ Navigate to Chapter 7 of the Student Resource Center.

   ▪ Open BusinessDisasterPlanningChecklist.pdf and read the content.

6. Read about risk analysis.

   ▪ Navigate to Chapter 7 of the Student Resource Center.

   ▪ Open Risk Analysis.pdf and read the content.

Chapter 8

Network Vulnerability Assessment

Objectives

After completing this chapter, you should be able to:

- Understand vulnerability assessment services
- Identify the sources of vulnerabilities
- Understand the methodology of network vulnerability assessment
- Select and use the right vulnerability assessment tool

Key Terms

Bug   an error in a piece of software after it was released by the vendor

Vulnerability   any weakness in a computer system that can be exploited to compromise the system's security

Introduction to Network Vulnerability Assessment

Any weakness in a computer system that can be exploited to compromise the system's security is considered a *vulnerability*. Vulnerabilities include anything from a weak password on a router, to a programming defect, to an open system service with a backdoor for hackers. Vulnerabilities open paths for worms, spyware applications, and e-mail viruses, making them the prime concerns of security consultants.

Vulnerability assessment is the process of identifying and logging these vulnerabilities. This helps in understanding and resolving problems before the vulnerability can cause any damage. Vulnerability assessments also help to validate security measures. If a user has recently installed an intrusion detection system (IDS) and it does not respond to one or more of the vulnerabilities discovered in the assessment, it may need to be reconfigured.

This chapter teaches you how to perform network vulnerability assessment.

Vulnerability Assessment Services

Vulnerability assessment services are used to scan a network's perimeter or demilitarized zone (DMZ) to identify known vulnerabilities and security weaknesses. These services can be scheduled by a user or by vendors to run automatically, or a private consulting firm can be hired to oversee the entire process. Vulnerability assessment services generally do not require advanced, powerful hardware to run.

Some advantages of vulnerability assessment services are:

- Provide a unique approach for identifying vulnerabilities
- Use a complete toolkit containing a combination of commercial products, modified open-source tools, proprietary tools, and modifications of commercial products
- Perform active probing, network view (remote testing), and host/server view (local testing)
- Used by different organizations according to the nature of their customers or their business partners
- Identify the security vulnerabilities that can compromise the client's information

Network Vulnerability Assessment Timeline

The network vulnerability assessment (NVA) may take as long as 12 weeks. The network vulnerability assessment process produces a detailed report showing the network's data and resource vulnerabilities.

The recommendations made by the network vulnerability assessment include:

- Policy and procedures modifications
- Architecture and topology changes
- Possible security hardware and software implementation recommendations

Network Vulnerability Assessment Team

A network vulnerability assessment team should contain at least one representative for each of the following areas:

- Information protection
- Operations
- Telecommunications
- System support
- Network management
- Desktop deployment
- Account administration
- Auditing

The team should be organized based on the following hierarchy:

- Sponsor (generally senior management)
- Team lead
- Policy review lead
- Policy review support
- Technical review lead
- Technical support

Members from these departments should also function as members of the NVA team:

- Physical security
- Facilities management
- Human resources
- IT security

Vulnerability Types

There are two major types of vulnerabilities: hard and soft. Hard vulnerabilities are problems with software after it is released by the vendor. These types of susceptibilities are usually called *bugs* and are resolved with patches and service packs. Keeping up with patches can be challenging and adds complexity to a system. It can also increase the quantity of services running on the system, slowing down operations.

Soft vulnerabilities include configuration errors in systems and the network. These errors are primarily due to human error and poor security management, and must be addressed quickly. The following can lead to soft vulnerabilities:

- Lack of organizational security policies and regulations
- Failure to account for security while outsourcing IT services
- Lack of security awareness training for all levels of staff
- Poor account management or password management by all users
- Poor physical security
- Weak configuration management practices that allow for vulnerable configurations
- Lack of vulnerability management practices that require system administrators to quickly correct critical vulnerabilities
- Failure to use strong encryption when transmitting sensitive information
- Insufficient monitoring and auditing practices

Goals of Vulnerability Assessment

There are two major objectives of the NVA. The first objective is to verify all aspects of the implemented security solutions. Because the entire security domain is transparent to the user, it must be tested exhaustively. This can take a good amount of time, but a single missed vulnerability can cause extraordinary damage.

The second objective is to generate a complete and concise report. NVA tools must be configured to generate reports that meet the organization's specific needs; the default parameters for report generation may not provide all the necessary information. A common NVA report starts with a one-page chart summarizing the state of the security measures.

Threat Management

Threat management involves actions taken to stop or prevent spyware, viruses, and other attacks. Intrusion detection systems (IDS) are a good solution for threat management. These systems monitor the network for intruder activity and generate logs when any such activity is detected.

Network Vulnerability Assessment Methodology

Network vulnerability assessment occurs over the following five phases:

1. Data collection
2. Identification
3. Analysis
4. Evaluation
5. Final report

Phase I: Data Collection

Once the NVA team has been formed, the team lead meets with management to discuss the scope of the assessment. The team leader will lay out a plan of how the assessment will take place and how that will affect business operations. It may be necessary to meet with network administrators and note their requirements. All comments from management and the IT team should be recorded.

The team should generate a list of the hardware and software in use, and then research the known vulnerabilities for every item on that list. All of these vulnerabilities must be tested in the next phase.

The following should be identified in this phase:

- Network
  - Identify network elements.
  - Identify routers, terminal servers, bridges, and hubs used for network connections.
  - Identify management systems used to monitor the network.
  - Determine network services.
  - Generate exception reports for delays in input or output.
- Hosts
  - Determine the critical host systems.
  - Determine the configuration of each host.
  - Determine software installed on the host.
  - Identify network services provided or used by each host.
- Applications
  - Identify the critical applications that are part of the assessment, including any major applications that are executed on the hosts identified previously.
  - Determine the criticality of the applications and the information that is used by these applications.
  - Identify if the applications are host based or work in a client-server environment.

In addition, all documents pertaining to the following are gathered:

- Network topology
- Firewall architecture
- Security mechanisms
- Databases
- Confidential information
- Information security policies
- System access policy and procedures
- IS infrastructure
- Detailed system list
- Methodology/SDLC

Phase II: Identification

The identification phase includes the following activities:

- The NVA team leader delegates the tasks and duties for further data collection.
- The NVA team leader prepares the agenda for interviews with the employees of the organization.
- The client organization makes arrangements for interviews and provides office space for them.
- NVA team members conduct the interviews of selected employees.
- The NVA team conducts vulnerability assessment tests on all operating systems, hardware, software, and network devices listed in the checklist generated in Phase I.

Interviews are conducted with the major communications facility support staff, customers, and other third parties working with the organization. People from the following departments must be interviewed:

- System and network administrators
- Support services (customer support, technical support, and help desk support)
- IT security

It is important to make the interviewees feel at ease. Interviewers should make sure the interviewees know that the network is being investigated, not the people; no one is on trial. Important topics for the interviews include:

- The background of the employee and his or her relationship with the network
- The data the employee traffics and how those data are handled
- The important data assets the employee uses
- The employee's understanding of the company's policies
- Any security weaknesses of which the employee is aware
- Any suggestions the employee has to enhance the company's security

Phase III: Analysis

The goal of the analysis phase is to detect vulnerabilities, implement countermeasures, and give suggestions to reduce risks. During this phase, the NVA team will:

- Run vulnerability analysis tools
- Verify results
- Determine potential defense mechanisms that can be applied to close discovered vulnerabilities
- Perform a risk analysis, estimating the potential monetary loss due to exploited vulnerabilities
- Evaluate the organization's security policy for completeness

Phase IV: Evaluation

The consequences of the investigations and findings should be documented in the draft report. The sponsor must review this report, and if any important changes are necessary or any further study is required, the draft will be revised and reviewed again. Anyone reading the final report should not see places where additional investigation should be done.

The following are the components of the report:

- Title page
- Information categorization
- Table of contents
- Executive summary
- Procedure overview
- Security profile
- Evaluation
  - Conclusion
  - Summary table of risks
  - Appendices

Phase V: Generation

The team lead gathers the sponsor's comments and combines them into the final report. The final report is in the same format as the draft report. Each copy should be numbered, to make it easier for the client to track all copies. The NVA team will keep one copy and pass the rest of the copies to the client. The team lead should be ready to discuss the plan for closing the discovered vulnerabilities.

Vulnerability Assessment Tools

Vulnerability assessment tools efficiently scan networks for any kind of vulnerability or breach in security policy. These tools can be configured to automatically scan the network, or they can be triggered manually as needed. They can also warn and alert the administrators in the event of an attack attempt, and take immediate action to limit the losses due to the attack.

Vulnerability assessment tools can be classified as one of the following:

- *Host-based tools*: Host-based vulnerability assessment tools are recognized by the host's operating system and test that system for vulnerabilities. These tools deal with general applications and services. They use the IP address of a particular host or a subnet range of hosts.

- *Windows-based vulnerability assessment tools*: These assessment tools are specific to Windows operating systems. They scan for vulnerabilities in the Windows OS and in Windows software.

- *Password vulnerability assessment tools*: Password tools check the strength of passwords. These tools themselves attack the passwords by guessing at them repeatedly and seeing if a weak password works. Many Windows-based vulnerability tools include password-checking features.

- *Application-layer vulnerability assessment tools*: These assessment tools work on servers and databases. Web server vulnerability assessment tools typically focus on widely used servers such as IIS, Apache, and iPlanet. Database vulnerability assessment tools check for strongly configured user accounts as well as the security of information and passwords stored in databases.

The following points should be kept in mind while choosing a security assessment tool:

- Specify the goals for the tools. What should they accomplish?

- Freeware and open-source tools should be used when possible in order to reduce costs. Open-source tools also have the advantage of being extremely configurable by computer programmers, if there is one on the team.

- The tools should present reports in complete and easily readable formats.

SAINT

SAINT gives accurate descriptions of all network vulnerabilities it finds, along with references such as Common Vulnerabilities and Exposures (CVE), CERT advisories, and IAVA (Information Assurance Vulnerability Alerts). It also suggests ways to reduce vulnerabilities, including available patches.

A SAINT scan occurs over three steps:

1. SAINT screens every working system and network device for TCP and UDP services.

2. SAINT performs checks to detect any vulnerabilities in those services.

3. After detecting the vulnerabilities, SAINT groups the results according to their criticality, type, or frequency of occurrence.

Benefits of using SAINT include:

- Helps in prioritizing threats to invest resources in the most important issues

- Helps quickly detect vulnerabilities

- Is easy to configure and manage

Nessus

Nessus is a comprehensive, flexible, open-source vulnerability-scanning program using a client-server architecture. This tool identifies open ports and then attempts to exploit them using user-written tests in NASL (Nessus Attack Scripting Language). The scan results can be presented in different formats including plaintext, XML, and HTML. Scanning can be automated using a command-line client. In addition to checking network vulnerabilities, Nessus can check passwords using dictionary and brute-force attacks. The program even allows its activities to be hidden from network intrusion detection systems (NIDS).

Some features of Nessus include:

- Smart service recognition (will identify an FTP or HTTP service on a nonstandard port)

- Tests multiple instances of the same service on each device

- SSL support

- Large user base

- Tested and proven on huge networks

BindView

BindView tests operating systems, software, and databases for vulnerabilities. It scans the vulnerabilities according to their priority and presents them in an easy-to-understand form, providing complete details of any detected vulnerability.

The main functions of BindView include:

- Detects all equipment deployed across the network, including devices that may not be considered useful
- Assesses threat levels
- Generates alerts for security issues
- Can be configured to correct some errors automatically
- Includes integrated reports such as SANS Priority One, CGI Banner exams, and RPC scanner reports
- Comes with certification programs customized for different purposes
- Includes a content database that maintains an easily accessed record of detected vulnerabilities

Nmap

Nmap is an open-source vulnerability assessment tool. It includes both console and graphical versions, and works with large networks or single hosts. Nmap works with many operating systems, including Windows and Linux, and includes up-to-date white papers and tutorials.

Ethereal

Ethereal is a GUI network protocol analyzer. It displays the active data packets captured from an existing live network or from a stored file of previously captured data packets. Ethereal can read and import the following file formats:

- Libpcap, Tcpdump, and various other tools using Tcpdump's capture format
- Snoop and atmsnoop
- Shomiti/Finisar Surveyor captures
- Novell LANalyzer captures
- Microsoft Network Monitor captures
- AIX's iptrace captures
- Cisco Networks NetXray captures
- Network Associates Windows-based sniffer captures
- Network General/Network Associates DOS-based sniffer (compressed or uncompressed) captures
- AG Group/WildPackets EtherPeek/TokenPeek/AiroPeek/EtherHelp/PacketGrabber captures
- RADCOM's WAN/LAN analyzer captures
- Network Instruments Observer version 9 captures
- Lucent/Ascend router debug output
- Files from HP-UX's Nettle
- Toshiba's ISDN router dump output
- The output from i4btrace from the ISDN4BSD project
- Traces from the EyeSDN USB-S0
- The output in IPLog format from the Cisco Secure IDS
- Pppd logs (pppdump format)
- The output from VMS's TCPIPtrace/TCPtrace/UCX$TRACE utilities
- The text output from the DBS Etherwatch VMS utility
- Visual Networks' Visual UpTime traffic capture
- The output from CoSine L2 debug

- The output from Accellent's 5Views LAN agents
- Endace Measurement Systems' ERF format captures
- Linux Bluez Bluetooth stack hcidump -w traces

Ethereal will read any of these files and automatically determine their format, and it can read files directly from gzip archives.

Retina Network Security Scanner

Retina Network Security Scanner detects known security vulnerabilities and aids in prioritizing threats. It features high-speed, accurate, and nonintrusive checking, allowing users to protect their networks against revealed vulnerabilities. Retina can also impose standards-based registry settings via custom policy audits. The majority of Retina scans can be performed without administrator rights. At the beginning of each session, Retina automatically downloads an updated vulnerability database.

Sandcat

The Sandcat scanner for Windows scans Web applications based on the SANS Top Twenty List of Critical Network Susceptibilities, developed in collaboration with the FBI's National Infrastructure Protection Center. It supports HTTPS (SSL) and the Common Vulnerabilities and Exposures (CVE) standards. Sandcat's key features include:

- Offers more than 56,000 security checks for the top Web server platforms
- Scans local or remote servers
- Executes destructive and nondestructive scans, and analyzes intrusion detection systems
- Supports OSVDB, NVD, and CVE, and filters false positives
- Automatically investigates and evaluates the server's configuration to assess which tests are required
- Incorporates a baseline security scanner that guarantees security against outdated server software

VForce

VForce is a scanner built to check custom Web applications. Its features include:

- Checks for buffer overflows, cross-site scripting, and SQL injection
- Modification of all HTTP requests (user-agent, cookies)
- Brute-force tests to locate weak passwords
- Programmed, domain-spanning page requests/downloads/availability tests
- Interoperability with HTTP
- Automatic records of tests
- Designed to locate new vulnerabilities in conventional applications
- Selective scans locate pages and patterns
- Computes the impact on the test system

ScanIT Online

ScanIT Online is an online vulnerability scanner that nonintrusively checks for vulnerabilities on any remote target with an IP address. It also collects data on the target including operating system types and open ports. Its reports prioritize vulnerabilities and describe solutions for patching the vulnerabilities.

Chapter Summary

- Any weakness in a computer system that can be exploited to compromise the system's security is considered a vulnerability.

- Vulnerabilities open paths for worms, spyware applications, and e-mail viruses, making them the prime concerns of security consultants.

- There are two major types of vulnerabilities: hard and soft. Hard vulnerabilities are problems with software after it is released by the vendor. Soft vulnerabilities include configuration errors in systems and the network.

- Network vulnerability assessment occurs over the following five phases: data collection, identification, analysis, evaluation, and final report.

- Vulnerability assessment tools efficiently scan networks for any kind of vulnerability or breach in security policy.

Review Questions

1. What is vulnerability assessment?

_____

_____

_____

_____

2. What is the difference between hard and soft vulnerabilities?

_____

_____

_____

_____

3. What are the goals of vulnerability assessment?

_____

_____

_____

_____

4. What are the features of a good vulnerability assessment?

_____

_____

_____

_____

5. What are the five phases of network vulnerability assessment?

_____

_____

_____

_____

6. What is a vulnerability assessment tool?

_____

_____

_____

_____

7. How are vulnerability assessment tools selected?

_____

_____

_____

_____

8. What are a few vulnerability assessment tools?

_____

_____

_____

_____

_____

Hands-On Projects

1. Use Nmap for security auditing.

   ■ Navigate to Chapter 8 of the Student Resource Center.

   ■ Install and launch the Nmap Umit program.

   ■ Select a target and a profile and click **Scan**.

   ■ The scan report will appear.

2. Use Retina Network Security Scanner to scan a network.

   ■ Navigate to Chapter 8 of the Student Resource Center.

   ■ Install and launch the Retina Network Security Scanner program.

   ■ Check any desired check boxes in the Select Options list.

   ■ In the Target Type drop-down menu, select **Single IP** and type the target's IP address.

   ■ Type the filename and job name.

   ■ Click **Scan**.

   ■ Check the results after completing the scan.

   ■ For a particular range of IP addresses, under Target Type, select **IP Range**.

   ■ Type the range of IP addresses and click **Scan**.

   ■ Click the **Discover** tab.

   ■ Select the **Report** tab and click **Generate** to create a report.

   ■ To view the report in Microsoft Word, click the **Microsoft Word** icon.

   ■ Click **Schedule** to schedule an automated scan.

3. Use the Nessus tool for vulnerability scanning.

   ■ Navigate to Chapter 8 of the Student Resource Center.

   ■ Install and launch the Nessus program.

- Select **Start Scan Task.**
- The next screen will prompt for an IP address or range of IP addresses. Type the internal IP address **127.0.0.1** and click **Next.**
- Select the **Enable all but dangerous plugins with default settings** option and click **Next.**
- To scan from a remote server, select **Scan from a remote Nessus server** and fill in the remote server's name or IP address, username, and password. Otherwise, select **Scan from the localhost.**
- Click **Scan now** to start the scanning process.

4. Use Security Manager Plus to detect vulnerabilities.

- Navigate to Chapter 8 of the Student Resource Center.
- Launch the Security Manager Plus program.
- Type a username and password and click **Login.**
- Click **New Scan** and then **Scan Network.**
- Type the target IP address or range.
- Click **Scan Now.**
- Click **Assets** to see the scanned ports.
- Select any asset to view the results.
- Click the **PDF** icon to generate a report in PDF format.

5. Use Shadow Security Scanner to provide a secure, prompt, and reliable detection of a vast range of security system holes.

- Navigate to Chapter 8 of the Student Resource Center.
- Install and launch the Shadow Security Scanner program.
- Click **File** and then **New Session.**
- Select the **Complete Scan, Full Scan,** or **Quick Scan** rule.
- Type the description of the session and click **Next.**
- Click **Add host** and click **Next.**
- Type the IP address or hostname and click **Add.**
- Click **Start scan.**
- Click the **Vulnerabilities** tab to view any vulnerabilities found.
- Click **IP address** to see the different types of vulnerabilities.
- Save the session.
- Click **Options** to view other options.
- Click **General** to change the speed, modules, total threads, ping timeout, and data timeout parameters.
- Click **Scanner** to change scanner parameters.
- Click **Scheduler** to schedule the scan.
- Select the **When to start** tab to set the time and date.
- Select the type of scan and give it a name.
- Add a host and click **Add.**
- Select the day of the week to perform the scan.
- Click **Exit** to close the application.

A

Address list, 2-6

Adobe Reader, 1-15

Adobe Shockwave and Flash, 1-15

Apple QuickTime, 1-15

Archiving, 5-12

ARP spoofing, 1-7

Artifact, 6-13

Asymmetric-key encryption, 3-6, 3-7

Asynchronous systems, 7-3

Attachments, 2-1, 2-6, 2-18–2-20

Authentication, 3-2

Authentication header (AH), 3-10

Authentication techniques, 1-10–1-11

Authentication tokens, 3-2

B

Backup, 5-5–5-6, 7-2–7-4

BCArchive, 2-22

BlindView, 8-7

Bots, 1-4

Browser behavior analysis, 1-14

Browser hijacking, 1-12–1-14

Browser security, 1-12

Browsing analysis, 1-11–1-12

Buffer overflow, 1-5

BugMeNot, 1-16

Bugs, 8-3

Bump in the Stack (BITS), 3-11–3-12

Business continuity planning, 7-2

Business impact analysis (BIA), 7-11

C

CenturionMail, 2-7

Certificate authorities, 1-8

Cipher Block Chaining (CBC), 3-8

Cipher Feedback Mode (CFB), 3-8

Ciphertext, 3-3

Circuit redundancy, 5-12

Client authorization

authentication techniques, 1-10–1-11

certificate authorities, 1-8

client-side data, 1-8–1-9

input data validation, 1-11

server-side data, 1-9–1-10

user approaches, 1-10

Client-server architecture, 2-15

ClipSecure, 2-21

Clustered servers, 5-10–5-11

Common Gateway Interface (CGI), 1-16–1-19

Compulsory tunneling, 4-4

Computer security incident response team (CSIRT), 6-11–6-14

Concentrators, 4-7

Connectivity, 1-7

Containment, 6-9

Content spoofing, 1-5

Cookies, 1-9

Cross-site request forgery (XSRF or CSRF), 1-4

Cryptainer LE, 2-22

Crypto Anywhere, 2-21

CWShredder, 1-12, 1-13

D

Data Encryption Standard (DES), 3-7–3-8

Data files, 1-9

Deployment testing, 5-12

Detection, of incident, 6-8

DHCP (Dynamic Host Configuration Procotol) server, 4-12–4-13

DHCP (Dynamic Host Configuration Procotol) service, 4-9, 4-11

Diffie-Hellman encryption, 3-8, 3-9

Digital certificates, 3-15–3-16

Digital signatures, 3-16–3-17

Disaster recovery

introduction, 7-1

myths about, 7-11–7-12

overview, 7-2–7-4

planning, 7-4–7-7

Disk striping, 5-8

Disk striping with parity, 5-8

Distributed denial-of-service (DDoS) attacks, 1-3

DNS attack, 1-5

DNS cache poisoning, 1-7

Dynamic code, 1-14

E

Earthquakes, 5-4

Electronic Codebook Book (ECB), 3-8

E-mail

bombing, 2-20

client-server architecture, 2-15

components of, 2-3–2-6

configuring and testing a server, 2-7

configuring Outlook Express, 2-13

elements of, 2-2

encryption and authentication, 2-7–2-8, 2-9

POP3 vs. Web-based, 2-2–2-3

protocols, 2-13–2-15

Softalk WorkgroupMail, 2-9–2-13

tracking, 2-24

E-mail security

increasing, 2-20–2-23

introduction, 2-1

risks, 2-15–2-20

E-mail spoofing, 2-18

Encapsulating Security Payload (ESP), 3-11

Encryption

algorithms, 3-5–3-6

firewall implementation, 3-3–3-4

hashing algorithms, 3-5

maintaining confidentiality, 3-4

message authentication, 3-4

preserving data integrity, 3-4

scheme analysis, 3-6–3-10

strength, 3-5

Enterprise certificate authority, 4-11

E-pending, 2-15

Eradication, 6-10

Ethereal, 8-7–8-8

F

Failover clustering, 5-10–5-11

Fault tolerance

  deployment testing, 5-12

  introduction, 5-2

  planning for, 5-2

  preventive measures, 5-4–5-12

  reasons for system failure, 5-2–5-4

File synchronization, 5-12

Fire, 5-3

FTP bounce, 1-4–1-5

G

Gateway virus scanners, 2-17

GFI MailEssentials, 2-23

H

Hacking, 5-2–5-3

Hardware failures, 5-4

Hash encryption, 3-7

Hashing, 3-5, 3-7

Header, of e-mail, 2-3–2-6

Hidden files, 1-9

HMAC, 3-5

Hoaxes, 2-16

HTML Validator, 1-15

Hushmail, 2-8

I

IAS installation/configuration, 4-11–4-12

Identity theft, 1-2

Incident response

  approach to, 6-7–6-11

  architecture, 6-6–6-7

  classification of incidents, 6-1–6-2

  computer security incident response team, 6-11–6-14

  incident management, 6-6

  introduction, 6-1

  reporting incidents, 6-3–6-5

Input data validation, 1-11

Internet, client-server architecture in, 2-15

Internet Engineering Task Force (IETF), 4-5

Internet information services (IIS), 1-8

Internet key exchange (IKE) security associations, 3-14

Internet Message Access Protocol (IMAP), 2-14

IP address, 1-11

IPSec

  algorithms, 3-14

  components of, 3-12

  configuration, 3-13–3-14

  implementation, 3-11–3-12, 3-13

  limitations, 3-15

  modes, 3-13

  policies, 3-14–3-15

  processing steps, 3-14

  protocols, 3-10–3-11

IP spoofing, 1-6

J

Java, 1-15

K

Kerberos, 2-8

L

LAN, client-server architecture in, 2-15

Large-system recovery, 7-4

Layer two tunneling protocol (L2TP), 4-5–4-6

Load balancing, 5-11

Logical attacks, 1-5

M

MAC address, 1-11

Malware, 2-17–2-18

Man-in-the-middle attacks, 4-20

McAfee Stinger, 1-12, 1-13

MD5, 3-5

Message digest, 3-7

Microsoft Exchange 2000 e-mail server, 2-7

Mirrors, 5-8

Mozilla Firefox extensions, 1-15

Multihomed host, 4-4

Multipurpose Internet Mail Extensions (MIME)/Secure MIME, 2-14

N

Nessus, 8-6

Network access server (NAS), 4-4

Network addresses, 1-7–1-8

Network circuit failures, 5-4

Network recovery, 7-4

Network vulnerability assessment

  definition of *vulnerability*, 8-1

  introduction, 8-1

  methodology, 8-3–8-5

  services, 8-2–8-3

  tools for, 8-5–8-8

Nmap, 8-7

Novell GroupWise e-mail server, 2-7

O

Offsite storage, 5-7

Open Text, 1-16

Outlook Express, 2-13

Outlook viruses, 2-17–2-18

Output Feedback Mode (OFB), 3-8

P

Parasitic malware, 1-4

Parity bit, 5-8

PATH_INFO, 1-17

Perimeter security, 5-6–5-7

Phishing, 2-16

Physical security, 5-7

Plug-ins, 1-14–1-16

Point of presence (POP) server, 4-4

Point-to-point tunneling protocol (PPTP), 4-4, 4-5

POP3 e-mail, 2-2

Post Office Protocol Version 3 (POP3), 2-14–2-15

Power failures, 5-4

Power generators, 5-6

Pretty Good Privacy (PGP), 2-7, 2-8, 2-14, 3-8

Private-key infrastructure (PKI), 3-17

Public-key certificate, 3-16

Q

Quarantining e-mails, 2-20

QUERY_STRING, 1-17

R

Rainbow table, 3-5

ReadNotify, 2-24

Redundant array of independent disks (RAID), 5-7–5-10, 5-11

Remote access policy, 4-12

Restrictive access, 1-6

Retina Network Security Scanner, 8-8

Risk analysis

    introduction, 7-1

    methods of, 7-8–7-9

    potential threats, 7-8

    results evaluation, 7-11

    risk management, 7-9–7-10

    roles and responsibilities in, 7-10–7-11

Rivest-Shamir-Adelman (RSA) encryption, 3-8

Routing protocol spoofing, 1-6

Routing table poisoning, 1-7

RSA SecurID, 3-2

RSS/atomic injection, 1-5

S

Sabotage, 5-3

SAINT, 8-6

Sandcat, 8-8

ScanIT Online, 8-8

Secure Hive, 2-7, 2-8

Secure Multipurpose Internet Mail Extensions (S/MIME), 2-7

Secure Sockets Layer (SSL), 3-9–3-10

Security policy, 3-13

Server-side data, 1-9–1-10

Server Side Includes (SSIs), 1-18

Session hijacking, 1-4

Signatures, on e-mail, 2-6

Simple Mail Transfer Protocol (SMTP), 2-14

Simple server redundancy, 5-11–5-12

Small-system recovery, 7-3

Smart cards, 1-11, 3-2

Smurf attack, 1-4

Snarfing, 2-17

Social engineering, 6-8–6-9

Softalk WorkgroupMail, 2-9–2-13

Software failures, 5-4

Spam, 1-2–1-3, 2-15–2-16

SpamAware, 2-23

Split tunneling, 4-13

Stateless protocol, 5-11

Symmetric-key encryption, 3-6

Synchronous systems, 7-3

T

Tape autochangers, 5-5

Terrorism, 5-3

Threat management, 8-3

3DES, 3-8

Traffic-filtering devices, 1-8

Trojan horse (Trojans), 2-18

Tunneling, 4-2–4-6

U

Unauthorized network devices, identifying, 1-6–1-8

UNIX e-mail server, 2-7

UPSs (uninterruptible power supplies), 5-6

URLs, 1-9

US-CERT incident report forms, 6-5

User errors, 5-3

Username enumeration vulnerabilities, 4-18, 4-20

V

Validate CSS, 1-16

Validate Links (W3C), 1-16

Validate P3P, 1-15

Validate RSS, 1-16

Validate Sites HTML, 1-15

VeriSign Authentication, 3-2

VForce, 8-8

View-In, 1-16

Virtual private networks (VPNs)

    classification, 4-2

    connection, 4-7

    introduction, 4-2

    policies, 4-13

    product testing, 4-16–4-20

    security, 4-6–4-7

    server implementation, 4-9–4-13

    setting up, 4-7–4-9

    troubleshooting, 4-13–4-16

    tunneling, 4-2–4-6

Viruses, 2-17–2-18, 5-3

Voluntary tunneling, 4-3

VPN server, 4-12–4-13

Vulnerability, defined, 8-1

Vulnerability checks, 2-20

W

Water damage, 5-4

Web-based e-mail, 2-2–2-3

Webpage Speed Report, 1-16

Web security

    client authorization, 1-8–1-11

    Common Gateway Interface, 1-16–1-19

    common threats on Web, 1-2–1-6

    deploying and managing Web-based solutions, 1-11–1-14

    identifying unauthorized network devices, 1-6–1-8

    introduction, 1-1

    plug-ins, 1-14–1-16

    Web architecture, 1-1, 1-2

Windows Defender, 1-14

Windows Media Player, 1-15

Windows registry, 1-9

WORMs, 1-10

Worms, 2-18, 5-3

X

X.509, 3-8–3-9

X.509 authentication standard, 3-16